# PLAIN
# TALK
# ON

# Exodus

"Out of — Across — Into"

## MANFORD GEORGE GUTZKE
### PH.D.

**ZONDERVAN**
**PUBLISHING HOUSE** OF THE ZONDERVAN CORPORATION
GRAND RAPIDS, MICHIGAN 49506

# CONTENTS

# INTRODUCTION

The Bible tells us what God will do for any man who accepts Jesus Christ as Savior and Lord. This revelation is not presented in words only (whose meaning may change) but mainly in historical events (that cannot be altered).

In an event something happens, becoming actual. The Gospel tells about the work of Christ, wherein He did what was necessary for the saving of souls. Thus His coming, His life as Jesus of Nazareth, His death, burial, and resurrection, and His ascension to the right hand of God was an event in history with meaning for us all.

To enable us to grasp the meaning of Jesus Christ, the Scriptures recorded certain events in the history of Israel, which "happened to them for ensamples; and they are written for our admonition, upon whom the ends of the world have come." These recorded events were designed, reported, and interpreted to convey to our hearts the true meaning of the will of God.

The Book of Exodus records a major event in the history of the children of Israel that happened just one time. The whole nation was brought out of bondage into freedom by the guidance and the power of God. This is precisely what happens to the soul of any believer in the work of salvation.

Every human being begins living in this world as a natural person in bondage to sin. In His compassion and grace God sent His Son to redeem and to deliver sinners. By His power the Savior is able to bring the believer into the kingdom of God, where he can serve God and enjoy Him forever.

The whole operation of salvation is a movement *out of* bondage, *across* a temporary state of training, *into* the blessedness of freedom. These three phases can be identified in the Exodus of Israel as seen in the following diagram.

| EGYPT | DESERT | CANAAN |
|:---:|:---:|:---:|
| **"Out of"** | **"Across"** | **"Into"** |
| **BONDAGE** | **JOURNEYING** | **FREEDOM** |
| (Slaves) | (Pilgrims) | (Free Men) |

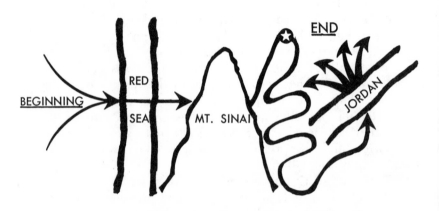

A General Overview
of
**THE PLAN OF SALVATION**

## Chapter 1

## THE PLAN OF SALVATION

Do you know why the result of the Gospel is called salvation?

> Brethren, my heart's desire and prayer to God for Israel is, that they might be saved (Rom. 10:1).

In these words the apostle Paul expressed his deep concern for the welfare of his kinsmen. Later he indicates how blessedness could be had by anyone:

> That if thou shalt confess with thy mouth the Lord Jesus, and shalt believe in thine heart that God hath raised him from the dead, thou shalt be saved (Rom. 10:9).

Peter was referring to this same truth when he said, "For there is none other name under heaven given among men, whereby we must be saved" (Acts 4:12). The word "saved" is a common word among believers generally. Whether we think of the word "saved" or the word "salvation," it is what we expect to hear in any church.

There are two worlds in the universe that we are in: the natural world that we can see, which we speak of as the earth; and the spiritual world, which we speak of as heaven, where God is. These are both real. Man lives and deals in both worlds. He lives in this world by using food and drink and shelter, which he gets out of this world's affairs, and he lives in the other world by participating in the Word of God, by receiving from God what He has to offer. He is in that sense a citizen of each. Man's outward actions are in this world: that is why we can see them; but what he actually amounts to and his destiny are in the other world that has to do with God. Natural actions occur here and we do them naturally. They may vary with different people,

11

but they all tend to serve self. From the time the baby first starts moving, and for as long as that child is living and is a natural person, it will reach out to get things for itself, which it will take to itself. The baby will try to keep for itself anything it wishes to have. That is natural.

Spiritual action — actions in the presence of God — all must be learned. The actions that we expect from a person who is a believer in Christ must be learned. They are in relation to God, who is invisible to the natural man. A person cannot possibly hear, understand, and imitate them. But spiritual living is quite possible: there are passages of Scripture that bear this out. For people who have received Christ Jesus as their Savior, yielded themselves to God, and received the Holy Spirit of God to dwell in them, there will be spontaneity within them so that without effort on their part they will do things that will be pleasing in the sight of God because the will of the Lord Jesus Christ is in them. This is the general condition of being "saved."

Let us look more closely at these two worlds. God made them both. He created the heavens and the earth. God made man with a body for this world and a spirit for the other. As Adam lived and became aware of himself he sinned. Right then a principle began to operate that is still true all across the board for all time: "The soul that sinneth shall surely die." To say that a soul shall "die" means that it will be ruined. When the first man, Adam, sinned as he did in the Garden of Eden, he brought all men who were his descendants into sin. Now a general statement of this sort may be made: man is born in sin, with sin, and is doomed to die and to be ruined. Paul points out that when sin entered the world death came because of sin, and because all men were involved in sin, so death came upon all men (Rom. 5:12). This meant not only death to their physical bodies but death to their spiritual beings. Man actually was separated from God because of Adam's sin.

We rejoice in the marvelous truth of John 3:16: "For God so loved the world, that he gave his only begotten Son, that whosoever believeth in him should not perish, but have everlasting life." Man will perish in his sin and he is condemned to die: but though he is doomed, yet God loved him. This word "love" does not refer to the way God felt. If there is any emotion on the part of God involved, it is compassion and pity. This word "love" is an action word. It is what I do. It is not how I feel. In other words, if I am going to love poor people, I do for them. If I am going to love sick people, I do for them. If I am going to love our children, I do for them. The extent to which I wisely and faithfully do is the extent of my love.

> Herein is love, not that we loved God, but that he loved us, and sent his Son to be the propitiation for our sins (I John 4:10).

In the marvelous verse "God so loved the world . . ." the "so" does not refer to His emotion; it refers to the following action: "He so loved . . . that He gave His only begotten Son." This verse also tells us why He gave Him, "that whosoever believeth should not perish but have everlasting life." It should be kept in mind that while Christ Jesus died for all men, it is not true that all men are saved. This can be seen in the very words ". . . whosoever believeth shall not perish but have everlasting life." As a matter of fact, the very next verse goes on to say that ". . . whosoever believeth not is condemned already." The sinner is not condemned because he does not believe; he was already condemned because he had sin in him and this condemnation was already there. Man does not have to do anything to be condemned.

Many years ago I heard Dr. R. A. Torrey preach a great message on "How to be Saved." It was a clear presentation of the Gospel outline. He told us at the end of the message, "I would think naturally that you would expect that the next time we meet, I would preach to you about 'How to be Lost.' I don't need to preach about that. You won't have to do anything. That is where you are now." I shall never forget the way he said it. Suddenly I knew it was true.

In my own case, when I first really looked at John 3:16 there came to my mind a simple question: Why? Why would He do that? I was not lovely in my own eyes but God is so pure: "He is of purer eyes than to behold evil";

He certainly could not like me. It is obvious I had this whole matter mixed up in my mind. Somehow it had seemed to me that John 3:16 meant that God so liked the world that this is what He did. But that is not true. As I continued reading the Scriptures I found out how God feels about the world: "God is angry with the wicked every day." That is clearly how He feels. But His action was that He gave His Son for men so that if anyone wanted to be saved, he could be saved. Why would He do this? Still later I learned in my experience, He did this because of His grace: "Grace that is greater than all our sins."

> For ye know the grace of our Lord Jesus Christ, that, though he was rich, yet for your sakes he became poor, that ye through his poverty might be rich (II Cor. 8:9).

Because God is just, He must punish sin with death. If God did not punish sin, the devil could laugh at Him. Because He is gracious and merciful He provides a substitute to bear the penalty of the sin that has been committed. As Judge, God assesses the penalty like a judge would assess a fine. In grace, God sends His Son to pay the fine, to redeem "whosoever will" from this penalty. Redeeming man from guilt, delivering man from sin, bringing man into eternal life is the work of salvation. That is what is meant by the Word. It is the work of God in Christ Jesus, by Christ Jesus, through Christ Jesus.

This work of God is available to all, to any, to "whosoever will believe." However it is operative, it actually functions, only with those who do believe. In order to believe, a man must hear the Word of God. There is a way to be saved: man must hear about that way, understand about that way, accept that way, and obey in that way, that he may be saved. This is the plan of salvation which is revealed in the Word of God.

*Hear*
*understand*
*accept*
*obey*

## Chapter 2

## THE SCRIPTURES AS REVELATION

Can you understand why a revelation from God would be necessary if men were to have the Gospel?

Salvation is commonly thought of as the work of God. By that is meant that it is something that God does quite apart from human action. To be sure it is done in man, and it is done to man, and it is done for man, but it is done by God. It is God who actually works to save the soul. When this work of God operates, it results in righteous action on the part of the believer, as he responds to the will of God. But Salvation gets started and moves on because it is God working in us "to will and to do His good pleasure" according to His promises.

The life that I have in my relationship with God, the experience I have when I trust in God, and the works I perform when I obey God are produced in me by the indwelling Lord Jesus Christ, who does, in Himself, the will of God. When Christ does the will of God in me, I find myself carried along in the will of God. The Lord Jesus told His disciples, "apart from me you can do nothing." But what God will do in and through and by Christ will always be by His grace and by His will.

No man by searching can find out God. Only God knows what He will do, so that what He will do is known only to Himself and to whomsoever He reveals it by the revelation of His will.

> For the scripture saith, Whosoever believeth on him shall not be ashamed. For there is no difference between the Jew and the Greek: for the same Lord over all is rich unto all that call upon him. For whosoever shall call upon the name of the Lord shall be saved. How then shall they call on him in whom they have

15

not believed? and how shall they believe in him of
whom they have not heard? and how shall they hear
without a preacher (Rom. 10:11-14)?

The soul must *hear* and *believe* what God means to do
in order to be saved by what God means to do. God has
revealed His will from time to time.

God, who at sundry times and in divers manners
spake in time past unto the fathers by the prophets,
hath in these last days spoken unto us by his Son
(Heb. 1:1-2).

Peter wrote ". . . holy men of God spake as they were
moved by the Holy Ghost" (II Pet. 1:21). This would
likewise be true of their writing. For this reason Paul taught
the Scriptures to those who listened to him preach, that
they might know what God promises to do.

How could any man know what God is doing?

Now all these things happened unto them for ensamples: and they are written for our admonition,
upon whom the ends of the world are come (I Cor.
10:11).

In these words Paul refers to things that happened to
Israel at the time of the Exodus from Egypt. At another
time he wrote:

For whatsoever things were written aforetime were
written for our learning, that we through patience
and comfort of the scriptures might have hope (Rom.
15:4).

In writing to Timothy, Paul noted the basic purpose of the
Scripture. This passage emphasizes the importance of reading and heeding the Scriptures. If any person wants to know
the will of God he should study the Bible.

But continue thou in the things which thou hast
learned and hast been assured of, knowing of whom
thou hast learned them; and that from a child thou
hast known the holy scriptures, which are able to
make thee wise unto salvation through faith which
is in Christ Jesus. All scripture is given by inspiration
of God, and is profitable for doctrine, for reproof, for
correction, for instruction in righteousness: that the
man of God may be perfect, throughly furnished
unto all good works (II Tim. 3:14-17).

In the passages noted above, Paul writes plainly to point out the functional significance of the Scriptures. It is clearly to be seen why the Scriptures were written. It is obvious we have them in our hands. Paul reminded Timothy that from a child he had known the holy Scriptures "which are able to make thee wise unto salvation." When a person is wise unto salvation he understands about it: he knows how it works. And yet to "know the Scriptures" means that just reading the Bible as so many words is not quite enough. The Bible will point the way, it is true; but what is actually needed is the working of God by His Holy Spirit in the reader. God will bring things to pass in the heart and mind of the believer who has been instructed by the Scriptures giving ideas of what God will do and how God

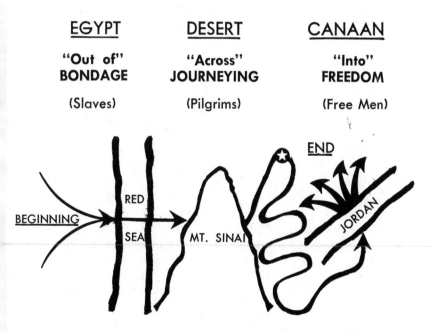

EGYPT      DESERT      CANAAN

"Out of"    "Across"    "Into"
BONDAGE    JOURNEYING   FREEDOM

(Slaves)    (Pilgrims)   (Free Men)

A General Overview
of
**THE PLAN OF SALVATION**

## THE PLAN

### Salvation Demonstrated in Exodus

| "OUT OF" | "ACROSS" | "INTO" |
|---|---|---|
| **NATURAL**<br>Kingdoms of Men | | **SPIRITUAL**<br>Kingdom of God |
| **EGYPT**<br>Worldly | **DESERT** | **CANAAN**<br>Heavenly |
| **ADAM** | **"CHRISTIAN"** | **CHRIST** |
| → | → | → |
| **"Come"!** | **"Abide"!** | **"Go"!** |

will do it. Thus the believer will be able to recognize what is happening in him. The Scriptures will make him wise unto salvation.

However just reading the words of Scripture alone will not be enough. Reading the text alone may make me wise enough and understanding enough so that I will turn to God to yield myself to Him. But when God works in me it is from the Scriptures that I will know what is happening. This truth can be illustrated by an incident in the life of the Lord Jesus Christ. Something happened on the day when He was raised from the dead that will help to show what I have in mind. On the evening of that day two of His disciples were walking from Jerusalem to their village Emmaus, talking over what had happened. Jesus of Nazareth met them as they journeyed. He had just been raised from the dead. He drew near and talked with them. Soon He discovered they were thinking about what had happened concerning the death of Jesus of Nazareth a few days before. Now they were walking along sad because He was gone.

I remember some years ago I wondered to myself as I read this account, why He didn't say, "Look at me." Why didn't He say, "Here I am. I am alive from the dead"? Then I realized they would not have understood what He meant. They could not possibly have grasped the truth of what they could see of His presence. The actual, physical presence of Jesus of Nazareth would not be enough. I have been profoundly impressed to note that He turned to Scripture to enable them to understand! He began with Moses and then the prophets to expound to them the Scriptures concerning Himself. It was when they heard the Old Testament explanation of the whole work of God in the resurrection that they were able to grasp the meaning of this person walking beside them.

It has always been amazing to me that although He was there in body, He did not use that fact to teach them. Later that night, when He was in the Upper Room with the disciples and was talking to them, He did use His body. He said, "Put your fingers in here. Handle me and see. A spirit hath not flesh and bones as you see me have." But that was in the context of their understanding of the Scriptures as He had been teaching them, and of all the things that happened on that road from Jerusalem. The truth is He helped them to interpret the meaning of His own resurrection body by using the Old Testament Scriptures.

You and I need to read and study the Bible in order to be able to understand what God is doing and what He will do.

> Search the scriptures; for in them ye think ye have eternal life: and they are they which testify of me (John 5:39).

Toward the end of that passage He said if they had believed the Old Testament Scriptures they would have known who He was:

> For had ye believed Moses, ye would have believed me: for he wrote of me. But if ye believe not his

writings, how shall ye believe my words (John 5:46-47).

If a person will not believe the Old Testament writings, he will not be able to believe the New Testament Scriptures.

The same truth is revealed in the story of the rich man in hell who asked that a messenger be sent back to his brothers that they should not come and be with him where he was. He was told, "They have Moses and the prophets; let them hear them. And he said, Nay, father Abraham: but if one went unto them from the dead, they will repent. And he said unto him, If they hear not Moses and the prophets, neither will they be persuaded, though one rose from the dead" (Luke 16:29-31).

The Scriptures are actually more significant for faith than the occurrence of miracles. We need to know what is in the Bible to understand what God has promised to do; and this is what we have in mind in the study of salvation. We will be studying the Old Testament Scriptures for the purpose of understanding the work of God in salvation.

*Chapter 3*

# THE SIGNIFICANCE OF OLD TESTAMENT SCRIPTURES

Do you realize that the Old Testament was written to reveal truth so that men might understand the life and work of Jesus Christ?

"We have found Him of whom Moses and the prophets did write." This is the way the early disciples spoke to one another; when they talked to one another in this way, they were referring to Jesus of Nazareth. He was the one of whom Moses and the prophets wrote. There are interesting aspects in the account given in the gospels. The writers did not make any reference to His appearance. There was nothing about the Lord Jesus Christ personally that would have given men any hint as to who He was. That is not how the disciples knew. They knew who He was because they knew what Moses and the prophets had written.

When reading the Bible to learn the truth of the Gospel of Jesus Christ, we do not find any description of Jesus of Nazareth. There is nothing recorded about His appearance. There was nothing about Him that, had you looked at Him and noted that, would have impressed you that this was the Christ. There was nothing described about His personal habits, His food, or His clothing; and yet salvation is provided for all who believe in Him. What, then, is the ground of our faith? We should admit at once that our faith is not grounded on what we think He looked like. And this fact will help us to say that the life of a believer doesn't depend upon what it looks like. That will help us to understand that, after all, there are people who can pretend and look as if they believed and yet not have real faith. This is not the source of saving faith. Faith in Christ is not based upon our judgment of Him as a human being; we do not know Him as a human being. We know that Jesus of Nazareth was the Incarnation of God. No one could know it by looking at Him. Thousands of people looked upon Him during the thirty years He lived, and none among them said, "I am impressed by your looks and I think you are the Christ." No. Yet there were some people who did know. Those who knew who He was were the people who knew the Old Testament Scriptures.

We are impressed to note that confidence in Him was not based upon His appearance, but upon His work. This is not only true about the person of the Lord; it is also true about works done in His name. As an illustration, let us consider a ten-dollar gift to the poor. Such a gift might not be given in the name of Christ. Such a gift need not necessarily be referred to as a Christian act. One could give a ten-dollar gift to the poor out of his own pity. There are people who are not believers in the Lord Jesus Christ who have compassion. When Paul was thrown on the Isle of Miletus, the record in Acts says the barbarians showed him no little kindness. You will find kindness, integrity, decency, and honesty among pagans, among people who do not profess any faith in God. This does not mean anything is misplaced. They are human beings; they happen to be good, just as others happen to be bad. But being good is not what makes them believers. Our interest is in salvation and we understand that salvation is the work of God through Christ Jesus, not through human virtue.

Then we may ask what does salvation mean? Salvation was promised in the Old Testament, and it was to be accomplished through a chosen one from God. The name that the Old Testament gave to this person was "Messiah," which in the New Testament language means "Christ." He was the anointed One. The Old Testament Scriptures promised that God would send Christ, who would save those who put their trust in Him. We read in John 5:39 that faith in Jesus Christ is only possible if you follow the Old Testament teaching. Without Old Testament promises, a person would not be able to believe in Christ. Jesus of Nazareth made all this very plain when He said:

> Search the scriptures; for in them ye think ye have
> eternal life: and they are they which testify of me.
> And ye will not come to me, that ye might have life.
> I receive not honour from men. But I know you, that
> ye have not the love of God in you. I am come in my
> Father's name, and ye receive me not: if another
> shall come in his own name, him ye will receive.
> How can ye believe, which receive honour one of
> another, and seek not the honour that cometh from
> God only? Do not think that I will accuse you to the
> Father: there is one that accuseth you, even Moses,
> in whom ye trust. For had ye believed Moses, ye
> would have believed me: for he wrote of me. But if
> ye believe not his writings, how shall ye believe my
> words? (John 5:39-47).

The general plan of what Christ would do when He came
to save His people was revealed in the history of Israel,
which was written for our guidance.

> Now all these things happened unto them for en-
> samples: and they are written for our admonition,
> upon whom the ends of the world are come (I Cor.
> 10:11).

So we study the Old Testament records to learn what happens in salvation. We start by studying the Old Testament
records to see who the Deliverer is, and we find that He is
Christ the Son of the living God, and that He is sent to save.

The story of deliverance in the Old Testament begins
with God's people in bondage in Egypt. Thus the whole
process, the whole program of salvation begins with man
being in a hole. It is common knowledge that man is in
trouble. Trouble in some cases is vulgar; in some cases it
is refined. Trouble in some cases is savage; in some cases
it is civilized. But one thing is sure: "man is born to trouble
as sparks fly upward." All men are in trouble. Every man
and every woman is in trouble. Sometimes we do not feel
our trouble so much. We are such strange human beings.
If we see that somebody else has more trouble than we
have, we do not feel so bad; but if we think we have more
trouble than anybody else, we feel just terrible. So often it
is so easy to arrive at this conclusion. Then we feel sorry
for ourselves. It is so easy to lament: "Nobody knows the
trouble I've seen."

In any case, no matter how one understands trouble or how one interprets or evaluates it, the fact of the matter is that God's whole program starts with the human soul in trouble, in bondage, as Israel was in Egypt. And the Hebrews were in distress. They were not only slaves in their society, but they were suffering as servants who were abused.

The next thing we see in Israel's history is that God saw the trouble they were in. He saw it and He sympathized with them. God showed that He is compassionate. Some people will say, "I don't understand how anyone can have the feeling of wanting to trust God and to serve Him. If God made this world with all the trouble that is in it, why did He do it?" I can't tell you why He made things as they are, but I can tell you one thing for sure, "He is touched with all the feelings of our infirmities." Whatever may be His reason and purpose (and I trust Him about that), I am confident He knew what He was doing and I believe He is doing something glorious. In the meantime, while we are here in bondage, we are in trouble, and we can hurt. He knows it and He feels it and He sympathizes with us.

When Jesus of Nazareth went to the grave of Lazarus with Mary and Martha, the record is that when He saw them weeping around the grave, "Jesus wept." The Lord Jesus knew what He was going to do. He knew He would raise Lazarus from the dead. He knew He would turn mourning into joy; but right then they were hurting. They were grieving and He grieved with them. His heart was touched with their feeling of their loss. Just so God sees the trouble that people are in.

God promised Abraham that His descendants would be delivered. He promised that in Abraham's seed all nations should be blessed. The promise that was given to Abraham and to his children was expanded to all people through the seed of Abraham. Even the Gentiles could put their trust in God, because when God sent His Son into this world to seek and to save the lost, He recognized no distinctions and no barriers of any kind. All men everywhere were to hear the Word: "Whosoever will may come." He had promised

Abraham that these children of his, who would be in trouble, should be delivered.

Then God sent a deliverer. God sent a person who was to bring them out. This was God's way of affecting their deliverance. At first Moses did not know the right way to do it; he did not recognize it. He went according to his own judgment. Even though he was the chosen one of God, and even though he was the one who would ultimately deliver them, he did not know the way God was going to do it. He tried to bring them out in his own wisdom and he failed. Forty years later he was sent back to bring them out in God's way; then he succeeded.

This is very significant to our study. God has His own way of delivering the human soul from trouble. The blessing that God wanted the Hebrews to have was not possible while they were in Egypt. This shows me that while I am in this natural world, in the situation that is giving me trouble, I will not be blessed. But the blessing will come to me when I die in this natural situation as it is and am raised from the dead in the newness of life. The work of God, His salvation, involves primarily a change of orientation, a change of relationship in the world in which I am living. In other words, as long as I am thinking of this natural world I will stay in trouble. Actually it is very reasonable that I should think of this natural world. I am in it. Everything I have is in it, and so naturally I think of it. But I am to learn from the history of Israel that if I think only of this world, I will never get out of trouble.

The way out of my trouble must be God's way. I must die in this natural world and so come out of its control. This is all set forth in His treatment of the children of Israel. All of the truth of God's work in salvation is pictured thus in the Old Testament Scriptures.

## Chapter 4

# THE WORK OF CHRIST IN SALVATION

Do you realize that the benefits of the Gospel of Christ Jesus are more important to us than anything else in the whole world?

One important aspect of the Gospel is that we learn from it that every benefit we receive is from Jesus Christ. Salvation is out in the open before our eyes. It has aspects that can be seen. When a person has peace of heart and mind, it shows in his countenance, in his whole manner: it can be noted in his quietness and assurance. There is no agitation, no depression, no irritation; there is acceptance of all kinds of disturbances. Such a person manifests longsuffering, gentleness, patience, and hopefulness. Such a person shows confidence in the outcome of anything in which he is involved. He is easy to talk to and is ready to support others as they go along in their fellowship with him. It is true that such an attitude as I have described, such a character as I have described, can be imitated. It can be simulated through will power, through self-control; even the imitation is pleasant to others and seems profitable although there is a hollow tone and an underlying strain in it.

When we find the true believer, the person who really knows the Lord Jesus Christ, we find one in whom there is to be seen and felt love, joy, peace, longsuffering, gentleness, goodness, faith, meekness, temperance. Although these appear in the man they are not by the man; they are not the result of his efforts. The common tendency among us is to praise such conduct. This reflects the common view that it was the person who did it; and so we give him credit for it. But this is not right. The person I described would be the first to tell you that he did not do it. He might even deny that it is true about him. He does not fully understand why it is that he feels personally so unfit and so weak while we give him credit for being strong. We give him credit for being wonderfully committed in his ways, even though he may not realize this is true.

We need to realize that what we see in that man is the fruit of the Holy Spirit of God and the result of Christ in him, the hope of glory. We need to keep in mind that as far as the life of the believer is concerned, the origin of that manner of life that he manifests is in the spiritual world, and the power that he maintains to live that way in spite of any circumstances is in the spiritual world. It is not his. He does not do it. Christ not only produces such consequences, He opens new possibilities. Paul, in writing about this, says:

> Therefore if any man be in Christ, he is a new creature: old things are passed away; behold, all things are become new" (II Cor. 5:17).

This spiritual living on the part of the believing person includes a turning to God: an open, honest repentance toward self; a new birth with interest in and acceptance of the Word of God, the promises of God; and the coming of the Holy Spirit into that person's soul. This is the sort of spiritual life I am talking about, and this sort of believing experience is inward. The world cannot see what is going on as a result of the Holy Spirit in the soul.

The ways of God are not to be seen by men, but the person in whom the Spirit is working, the believing person, will find in himself that he will be shown the things of Christ. As he lives he will be thinking and understanding about the things of Christ, and the Holy Spirit will enable him to respond in faith to the will of God. He will find in himself a readiness, actually an eagerness, to do God's will. The Holy Spirit will guide him into the will of God. He just wants the believer to know what God wants him to do and to be ready to do it. The Holy Spirit will comfort him and inspire him by showing him the work of Christ on his behalf. The Holy Spirit will make the believer fruitful. The Holy Spirit will actually affect him in such a way that as the believer lives along day by day he will show forth love, joy, peace, longsuffering, gentleness, goodness, faith, meekness, and self-control. He will not manifest one of these fruits because he tried to; these things will show up in him just as the petals of a rosebud show up in the rose, because the Holy Spirit activates in the believer the living will of the living Lord.

So far as we are concerned, we should be wise enough not to rely on our own strength. If someone were to say to me, "I think if a person is a believer he should try to be good." No doubt he means the believer should want to be good. I would agree. Perhaps he means the believer would like to have goodness throughout his life. I would agree with that also. But I am sure that if the believer understood what I am talking about he would know he could never do it. Then how would it ever happen? Let the Lord do it. The Lord can do these things. Believers should be wise enough not to rely on their own strength nor to rely on their own virtue. The first significant action on the part of Almighty God in salvation is to lead the soul into being spiritual, and thus to lift the person into spiritual living: that is, living in the presence of God. God does this by His own power and He will do this so that by His grace He will affect the believer that he will be enabled to respond to God and find himself doing things in obedience to God that he would not naturally want to do. The believer will find himself doing such things because he is led that way and strengthened that way. Moved by the Holy Spirit, he will find himself trusting God; he will believe in God more and more.

Every now and again I am distressed in my own heart when I find people who have difficulty trusting in God. The fact is that natural persons have difficulty believing in God. It is strange how many people feel that before they can trust God they must understand Him; and before they can believe in God they must understand what He is doing. Let me speak gently about this. No person will ever understand God. God is beyond any human mind, and for a person to stop everything until he understands God means that he is forever stopped. "The ways of God are past finding out." But a person can trust God: he can believe in God, because God is trustworthy.

If anyone wanted to know why he should trust God, I would say to him: "Look at Calvary's cross." Any person should trust God when he realizes that God gave His Son to die for him. That should be enough. There will be in me a readiness to believe in God and to trust God when I consider that He gave His Son to die for me. This is what the Holy Spirit will bring to pass. When I find myself trusting in God and believing in God, I will find that I love Him. Why? Because He first loved me. It will not be because I know so much about God; it will not be because I am intrigued by what I found out about God. I will have the joy of communion with Him. I will have the peace of God that passeth all understanding, because I remember that I am in His hands. As I live among others I will find that I am not irritable; I am not impatient with them, because I trust in God. My hope and my confidence are in God. I will have the gentleness of Christ in my heart, because He is so gentle with me. By walking in Him, having fellowship with Him, I will find that my conduct is such that people will say that I am good. That goodness is not mine; that goodness is His, and it is operative in me because I walk with Him. When I realize that He spared not His own Son but freely gave Him up for me, I can ask myself the question Paul asked, "How shall he not with him also freely give us all things?" (Rom. 8:32). I will be free from worry and uncertainty when I am sure that Almighty God is working all things together for good to them that love Him. I will have that disposition in me, because I am moved from within by the Holy Spirit of God to give God His due and to honor Him and to bow down before Him and to worship Him. That is the work of Christ in me. It is the work of Christ in salvation.

## Chapter 5

## THE FUNCTION OF FAITH IN SALVATION

Can you understand that faith requires action by the believer?

"For whosoever shall call upon the name of the Lord shall be saved." This is the way Paul expressed it, and when we look at that statement we can see there is an element in *believing* in the Lord that is more than simply *trusting* the Lord. A person could trust the Lord by accepting the course of events just as they are, and this could be very important. On the basis of that a person could have quietness and peace. To be sure "trust" is involved in "believing in," and in some ways it seems almost a prerequisite to "believing in." Trust is a blessing when one trusts in God. Trusting will enable a person to live in quietness and confidence.

But there is really no forward look in trust; it is more an upward look: the person looks toward God and trusts Him. But in believing, the person must expect something from God: there must be some revelation of a promise about something that God will do. In the original language "believing" requires some spoken word. Someone says something and the question then is: do you believe what he says? Believing anything is not valid. Some person may say rather naively, "I think that if you believe that is all that is necessary." If this were true it would appear that the actual believing, the action of believing, is the saving factor. But the Lord Jesus Christ is the saving factor: the death on the cross is the saving factor. Believing on my part is committing myself to Him; and that is necessary for me. I commit myself to Him. If I were to commit myself to someone else, there would be no salvation. I must commit myself to the Lord Jesus Christ.

God has revealed in the Scriptures His will to save people, to redeem them. He has revealed this in certain promises spoken to man. To take the promise as true, and to commit oneself to God in line with that promise, is action on the part of the believer. That is what is necessary. No doubt many persons remain in darkness of unbelief because they do not know what to believe. It is true that God is God, and they are subject to Him. They may recognize that, and in a vague sort of way they may fear God because they do not know what the future holds in store for them. This may all be true; and yet such a person would be helpless, so to speak, and would continue in a lost condition unless he knows what God is willing to do and what God wants him to do.

If a person does not know what God has promised, he cannot believe it. God is a living Being. The great truth in the Gospel is that God calls man to Himself. Each person needs to know the call of God and needs to hear this call in order to believe it. The fact is if he can believe it, he can have it. The Gospel presents the promise of God in Christ Jesus. When we think about the life of Jesus Christ on earth we remember that although He was abused yet He went about doing good. He told the truth about the meaning of Scripture; He died on Calvary's cross and was buried. Can you see in this the promise of God? Can you see how this reveals that He was the Christ, the chosen One of God: that He died for our sins (this is what promises forgiveness); that He was buried and He arose again the third day (which promises us new life); and that He was seen? This is the promise of God in Christ Jesus, and this becomes His call to me. When I hear these things about the Lord Jesus Christ, there is implied in them that which the Spirit will bring to my heart, this call "Come unto me." To respond to that call involves on my part a decision, a choice, to commit myself to Him. It is an inward thing, whether or not I actually trust in Him.

As you can understand by these words, the word "trust" is involved, but the action is what we mean by believing; and this involves obedience. He said, "Come." I need to obey. He said, "Look." I need to look. He said, "Hear." I need to hear. I need to do the things God asks me to do, and this obedience is the essential element in believing. If a person were to say that he believed in a certain cough medicine and if when he started coughing I asked if he had taken any medicine and he replied, "no," then I would say that in the strict sense of the language we are using, he did not really "believe" in it. If he believed in it he would have taken it. This is the way the Bible uses the word. When you say you believe in a doctor you go to him. If you believe in a certain mechanic who handles your car, you take your car to him. If you believe in the Lord as presented in the Gospel, you will obey Him.

To respond to the call of God involves a decision or a choice on my part. Perhaps someone may wonder "Why not?" The truth is that if I commit myself to Him, I will no longer be going my own way. I must yield to Him: I must take up my cross and follow Him. When He calls "Come unto me," I am to move in His direction. Moving means that I must let something go. I must turn away from some things. James, in speaking about this, has a plain simple word: "But be ye doers of the word, and not hearers only, deceiving your own selves" (James 1:22). It is most important to keep all this in mind as we try to understand the ways of God in salvation.

In the deliverance of the people of Israel out of Egypt there is the demonstration in history of the salvation plan of God. While the people originally were slaves they became free eventually, but they had to move. It was this initial commitment to God on their part, being willing to follow, which made their faith operative.

If on any day, at any point along the line, you and I wanted to decide whether we wanted the blessing of God, we would ask "What promise did He make?" Then we would face the issue, "Will we give ourselves over to that promise?" Such a commitment would always involve some aspect of denying oneself and turning to God, of letting go of oneself and giving oneself over to God. It is this initial commitment to God to respond to Him when He says, "Come," that counts in actually participating in the salvation process.

In practical situations this commitment is challenged. Suppose a situation arose where the believer was in real trouble; he would be facing a problem. What should he do? Should he yield himself at this point when his family might be involved or his job might be at stake or his career involved? It will help him if he will keep in mind "He that spared not His own Son, but delivered Him up for us all, how shall He not with Him also freely give us all things?" If the believer believes that Christ Jesus died for his sins, that He was buried, and that He arose again the third day for him according to the Scriptures, and that He was seen — if he believes that and commits himself to Him, salvation will be operative in that soul.

One word needs to be said here. God will give grace to enable a willing person to believe. If for any reason a person did not have the grace of God in his heart he could not believe what I have been talking about. But it is possible to have this grace if one will simply yield to God because He is gracious and He is anxious to help any person who wants to come to Him.

## Chapter 6

## NEED FOR SALVATION

Do you realize a person could live a normal human existence and never accept Jesus Christ as Lord?

> For if ye believe not that I am he, ye shall die in your sins (John 8:24).

It is a well-known fact that the Lord Jesus taught when He was here "you must be born again" and that He emphatically stated "apart from me (without me) you can do nothing." Many have stumbled at this point.

I can remember that when I used to read these words before I became a believer, I could not understand them at all. What did He mean, "without me you can do nothing"? I was a school teacher at the time. I had passed through high school, through normal training school as a teacher. I could handle things on the farm. I could do many things. I worked my problems in algebra and physics, and I could write my compositions in English. I could run my school and my affairs. So what did these words mean? For a long time I felt they were just an overstatement, a sort of exaggeration. The natural mind can easily fall into this error because the natural mind is thinking only of this world, or this life, and such was my case.

When thinking only of this world it is literally impossible to be born again. This was Nicodemus' problem. How can a man be born again? When I read that story the one line that made sense to me was, "How can a man be born again when he is old?" For Jesus of Nazareth to say, "Without me ye can do nothing" seemed a strange utterance in view of the achievements of the natural man. That implies that all literature ever written is nothing — that is, when written by men who were not believers in Christ. It would be the same with all paintings, works of sculpture, feats of engineering.

The truth is that all the works of the flesh, the works that man can do in himself, whether in government or in art or science — all such works of the flesh belong in this world. And this means that every one of them will perish. In these days some new discovery is reported almost every month, as when some travelers have come across a spot in the ancient world where there is evidence of a civilization older than ours. It has been fascinating to read of the great civilizations that were in South America and in Central America, before the white man came to this western hemisphere. But when we read about things that are happening in the Near East and the things uncovered by archaeologists as they go into these discoveries, or when we study such an obvious structure as a pyramid or the Sphinx, we can have one thought in mind: all these things will be ruined. None will last for eternity.

So far as this world is concerned, my life, my home, my work, everything amounts to nothing. In Matthew 24:1, 2 we read, ". . . and his disciples came to him for to show him the buildings of the temple (probably the greatest building in Jerusalem at the time). And Jesus said unto them, See ye not all these things? verily I say unto you, There shall not be left here one stone upon another, that shall not be thrown down." And this can be said of everything I have said so far: the works of man will not last. That is all there is to it.

If this world were everything that would be a different story; but if it is true that eternal life is real and there is another world after this, and that man should get himself ready for that world, then we can quickly understand that what we do here isn't going to count there.

I remember reading of the following incident. At a certain court dinner the emperor had his leading men and his military, financial, political, and religious leaders all present. In the seating of the guests a certain great military man, a general in charge of the military forces of Prussia at that time, was seated beside the court chaplain. Since this general was seated beside the chaplain he felt it incumbent upon him to be gracious and kind, so he turned to the chaplain and said, "Pastor, can you tell me anything about heaven?" And the chaplain simply said, "Well, I can't tell you much. We don't know what it looks like but I can tell you one thing for sure: you won't be a general there." That is true. The achievements of man will not count over there.

In Hebrews 9:27 occur these simple words, "It is appointed unto men once to die." It is not only true that the works of man will not last, but the life of man will not last. To be sure, in this world the natural man is busy, ambitious to do many different things and to achieve much in the way of personal work, but Christ Jesus did not come to do anything here. He did not even come to help others do anything here and when He said, "Without me you can do nothing," He was not talking about this world. By the way, this can be a real guide in the matter of praying. A great many people make requests for prayer that are entirely located in this world. I don't doubt that God can be kind and gracious as far as this world is concerned, but that is not the basic thing that Christ Jesus came to do. The promises of God point toward the kingdom of God. The kingdom of God has to do with that relationship with God wherein I obey Him: when I say "He is my King."

"For the kingdom of God is not meat and drink; but righteousness, and peace, and joy in the Holy Ghost" (Rom. 14:17). Thus we can recognize that the kingdom of God is not of this world, and we should remember it was about a person entering into the kingdom of God that Jesus of Nazareth said "except a man be born of water and the spirit, he cannot enter the kingdom of God." Paul states this in so many words, "Now this I say, brethren, flesh and blood cannot inherit the kingdom of God." It is enough just now for us to realize, so far as the kingdom of God is concerned, that all have sinned and come short of the glory of God. Remember, there is no man that sinneth not, and so no man in himself can qualify to enter the kingdom of God.

Under these circumstances we might ask, "What, then, can any man do?" And here is our message. The time is fulfilled. The kingdom of God is at hand. Repent ye and believe the Gospel. The sinner must believe in the Lord Jesus Christ. To belong to God as a child of God, a person must be saved. Before a person can do anything in the kingdom of God by obeying God it will be necessary for him to have the help of the Lord Jesus Christ. This is important to us as we study salvation as it is seen in the Exodus of Israel. As we look at that we shall find one truth that will come to us clearly: Israel would never have the blessing of God as long as they remained in Egypt. They cannot do it by themselves. They will have to come into the will of God.

For the Kingdom of God is not meat and drink, but righteousness and peace and joy in the Holy Ghost Rom. 14:17

## Chapter 7

## SALVATION IS BY THE GRACE OF GOD

Can you understand that the efforts and the achievements of a man are not adequate for his eternal salvation?

I hope no one will be unhappy when I repeat one truth over and over again: believers are saved by the grace of God. Even as a believer, I can't do it; I would not do it if it were in my hands. I will be saved by the grace of God exercised on my behalf in and through the power of the Lord Jesus Christ. The heart of man is vain. Jeremiah 17:9 says, "The heart is deceitful above all things, and desperately wicked." Do you know what that means? I can't trust me. I would be foolish to trust me.

It is easy for anybody to be deceived by his own wishes and by his own desires. This can be seen when human beings are called to put their trust in God. This was revealed in Old Testament times during the days of Israel in the writings of Moses.

> When thou hast eaten and art full, then thou shalt bless the Lord thy God for the good land which he hath given thee. Beware that thou forget not the Lord thy God, in not keeping his commandments, and his judgments, and his statutes, which I command thee this day: lest when thou hast eaten and art full, and hast built goodly houses, and dwelt therein; and when thy herds and thy flocks multiply, and thy silver and thy gold is multiplied, and all that thou hast is multiplied; then thine heart be lifted up, and thou forget the Lord thy God, which brought thee forth out of the land of Egypt, from the house of bondage (Deut. 8:10-14).

He warned them further:

> And thou say in thine heart, My power and the

38

> might of mine hand hath gotten me this wealth.
> But thou shalt remember the Lord thy God: for it
> is he that giveth thee power to get wealth, that he
> may establish his covenant which he sware unto
> thy fathers, as it is this day (Deut. 8:17-18).

It is revealing to note how Moses puts it: "Beware that thou
forget not the Lord thy God . . . lest when thou hast eaten
and art full . . . then thine heart be lifted up and thou forget the Lord thy God . . . and thou say in thine heart, My
power and the might of mine hand hath gotten me this
wealth." This could happen with believers today. A person
could be trusting in the Lord and be blessed, and then fall
into the temptation to think that he is strong enough to have
done this, good enough, and that he has earned it.

> And thou say in thine heart, My power and the
> might of mine hand hath gotten me this wealth.
> But thou shalt remember the Lord thy God: for it is
> he that giveth thee power to get wealth, that he may
> establish his covenant which he sware unto thy
> fathers, as it is this day. And it shall be, if thou do
> at all forget the Lord thy God, and walk after other
> gods, and serve them, and worship them, I testify
> against you this day that ye shall surely perish
> (Deut. 8:17-19).

That is how Moses warned about this whole matter. The
attitude that Moses referred to, which largely was a matter
of being in this world and being in the land of Canaan,
had to do with crops and cattle and herds. In our time this
attitude need not necessarily involve physical strength or
material benefits; it could occur in spiritual matters. A
believer could easily be deceived into thinking that some
spiritual victory, some spiritual achievement in his own
soul, was the result of his virtue and his faithfulness; and
thereby, he could forfeit his blessing. He could lose out
right there because he took the glory. All glory belongs to
God. This peril exists at all levels of scriptural experience.

For instance, how is one acceptable to God? If a person
is not careful in his natural heart and mind, he will think
"I will have to be good; I will have to do good: I will have
to avoid evil, etc." All such resolutions are good, but they
are not good enough. The soul is made acceptable because

a person believes in the Lord Jesus Christ. He is made acceptable in the Beloved. How does one come to God? The natural heart is not minded to come to God. To anyone who may be thinking of turning to God from an intellectual point of view, I would say as kindly but, I hope, as straightforwardly as I possibly could: "You do not have it in your heart to want to come to God. You do not have it in your heart to deny yourself."

How, then, does one serve God? Many people want to serve God by doing something for Him, by bringing in something to God, their money, their work, or something they have done. But that is not the way to serve God. A person serves God by worshiping Him. How can one do that? By having "Christ in you." I must be careful to point out that the actual performance of any spiritual exercise is by the grace of God in the heart through the indwelling Lord Jesus Christ. It is "Christ in you" that enables a person to serve God. The believer can serve God when he yields to the Son of God who serves Him perfectly.

How does one pray? All kinds of people are praying all through the Christian community, but how do they pray? A person prays acceptably to God by yielding to the indwelling Lord Jesus Christ and by letting the Holy Spirit within move him into the will of God. How does one yield to God? No one has it in him to do this. I don't have it in me. It is Christ in me who will do these things. How does one prove to be faithful? I don't have that kind of strength or that disposition. It is the grace of God in my heart that moves me this way. How does one trust God? The only way in which I can trust the invisible God is when the grace of God is given to me. In other words, He puts from Himself into my heart what I would call an enablement. He enables me to trust.

For instance, in talking to His disciples Jesus of Nazareth gave them some instruction along this line when He said these words,

> Behold, I give unto you power to tread on serpents and scorpions, and over all the power of the enemy: and nothing shall by any means hurt you. Notwithstanding in this rejoice not, that the spirits are sub-

ject unto you; but rather rejoice, because your names
are written in heaven (Luke 10:19-20).

This is something about which we could be joyful. Salvation includes the response of a changed life to do His will
so that the believer acts differently; he now shows love,
joy, peace, long-suffering, gentleness, goodness, faith, meekness, and self-control. When we realize that is what salvation means, it is obvious that the natural man is helpless.
He cannot do these things; in fact he does not want to do
these things. The natural man wants to change the world,
but he cannot do that. He wants to change himself, and
he cannot do that. Only God can help, and God does help
him as Paul writes, "By grace are you saved through faith
and that not of yourself."

Jesus of Nazareth said, "You must be born again." He
also said, "For God so loved the world, that he gave his
only begotten Son, that whosoever believeth in him should
not perish, but have everlasting life" (John 3:16). Salvation is glorious; it is wonderful. Just now I want to stress
it is God who does it. I want to emphasize it, and press it
into your soul. It is "Christ in you" that makes the difference.

Is He in you? If He is, certain things follow: you will
have the desire in your mind and heart to do God's will.
You won't have to make up your mind. It will be that way.
We shall learn in our study of Exodus that the Hebrews
needed to get out of Egypt, and they would get out because
God would bring them out. They could never have the
blessing of God while they stayed there, but they could
never get out by their own efforts. It was not something
they could do. Salvation is the work of God and it is free,
and this was what the Hebrews learned in the Exodus.

## Chapter 8

## SALVATION WAS PROMISED TO ABRAHAM

Can you see the importance of having the blessing of God demonstrated in the living experience of one man?

Living in this world is a real task. Things are not clearly identified. We do not know for sure what is what. Things are sometimes made easier and better but there will be other things that will hurt and make living barren, more dangerous and evil. Man is not born with knowledge. He does not know innately the what or how or when of life. He does not naturally have the strength to choose and to perform the wise thing. He needs help to know; he needs help to choose and to do. God knows. God understands and God can do. "For God so loved the world, that he gave his only begotten Son, that whosoever believeth in him should not perish, but have everlasting life" (John 3:16). This is man's greatest hope.

"For by grace (that is from God) are ye saved (that is in living) through faith (that is on our part)" (Eph. 2:8). But in order to believe there must be a promise revealed. A person must hear something before he can believe anything. If I am going to believe God I must hear the Word of God. Revelation of the Word of God is most effective for me when it is preached or presented through demonstration in some one person. A simple way to understand that is: I am just one person and if you are going to show me something that will affect me, it will be easier if you will show it to me in one person. It is very misleading when I listen to what happens to everybody and then somehow assume it will happen to me.

Consider something that happens to everybody. Everybody dies. That does not mean that I am dead; it does not

42

mean I am necessarily going to die today. If revelation is going to be effective in my life it must be presented to me as it would be demonstrated in one person. I am just one person. Things which are true for everybody do not help me much. Words alone are very uncertain and very inadequate. Words are difficult to understand and to imagine, to get into my mind. I need some actual demonstration.

The supreme revelation in the plan of God is that man will be saved by God Himself. Man is inclined naturally to think that if he is ever going to be saved, he will have to do it. But that is not true. In order to show man what He had in mind, God not only said certain things but He actually demonstrated in this way: He came into this world and became incarnate as man to show us. The incarnation was God's way. "God was in Christ reconciling the world to himself." This revelation of the plan of God to save men was primarily given to one man, to Abraham.

In a very real sense Abraham is the most widely recognized man in all history. To be sure he is not as great as Jesus Christ. As a matter of fact I would not compare Jesus Christ with anybody. But, other than Jesus of Nazareth, Abraham is probably the most widely recognized man. He is counted as the father of the three monotheistic religions, all of whom believe in one God: Jews, Christians, and Mohammedans.

What Abraham did in action and behavior can be recognized when it is contrasted with what the men of Babel did. The story of the men of Babel is in Genesis 11 and the story of Abraham begins in Genesis 12. The men of Babel said something like this: "Go to, let us make brick. Let us build a city. Let us make us a name lest we be scattered." All this was a very ordinary, human attitude. But Abraham "looked for a city which hath foundations whose builder and maker is God." Can you see the difference?

Paul tells us that Christ died for us, reconciling us to God, so that it would be possible that we who believe should receive the blessing of Abraham (Gal. 3:13-14). There is much in that sentence. Looking at it more closely reveals that Paul, in writing to the Galatian Christians, says that because Christ died for them, and because they believed in God through the Lord Jesus Christ and were reconciled to God, they would receive the blessing of Abraham, which is the promise of the Spirit through faith. When I first noticed that, I was startled. Nothing was mentioned of the Holy Spirit back in the Old Testament, at least not at that point and not in that way. So what would you think this meant? What is the promise of the Spirit? What happens when you have the Spirit? Isn't it true that you have fellowship with God, that He deals with you? And isn't that what Abraham wanted?

The record is that Abraham believed God: he obeyed Him. What needs to be spelled out here very slowly is that the believing Abraham did was actually demonstrated in his obedience. Believing in God begins by a consciousness of God. It is an awareness in the heart. It can be strengthened by the worship of God until it will become stronger and stronger, actually producing obedience to God. It will not be a matter of feelings; it will be in obeying God. It could be pointed out that it is impossible to believe while standing still, or while being preoccupied with one's own plans. If my heart and mind are full of what I am going to do, my talking about believing in God is just talk. It is not worth anything. If I am going to talk about believing God, He is a living Being and His hand is outstretched to me and if I am going to believe in Him, I will put my hand in His. If I am doing basically what God wants me to do, that is believing in Him.

Abraham's action is well known. He left his own country and went out, "not knowing whither he went." The blessing of Abraham was not in material things. Abraham did not believe in God in order that he might receive riches; he received them but that was not the reason why he obeyed. He believed in God that he might have fellowship with Him. He walked with God that he might be with God. This is the blessing of the Spirit. This blessing was promised to his seed: to Isaac, then to Jacob, and then to Christ, who is counted as the seed of Abraham.

The procedure to receive this blessing is classic. My soul looks up to God, wants communion with Him, seeks His will in practical matters, obeys what God wants me to do, and receives the Holy Spirit, and thus enjoys communion with God. This is "the blessing of Abraham."

*Chapter 9*

## SALVATION WAS DEMONSTRATED IN ISRAEL

Can you understand how salvation, which is promised in the Gospel, is not so much a change in personal attitude as it is a change in circumstances?

Our interest is in the whole matter of the salvation of the human soul. We begin by recognizing that men are in trouble. They are in distress. They must live in this world. Men normally face destruction, and the end of that is death. Even "the paths of glory lead but to the grave." It is then we remember the remarkable and wonderful statement that "God so loved the world, that He gave His only begotten Son, that whosoever believeth in Him should not perish, but have everlasting life." What we have here is a direct promise that for anybody who will believe in the Lord Jesus Christ, salvation is assured.

As we try to understand the meaning of this, let us picture something like this: let us say that a boy is floundering around in a lake, drowning. Some of the rest of us are, as it were, standing by. What shall we do? Shall we drain the lake or shall we deliver the boy out of the lake? The answer is not difficult. Let us look at another situation where a house is burning and a little girl is on the second floor. What shall we do? We would not want to leave her there. Somebody might say, "Put the fire out." Someone else would say, "Rescue the girl." The situation is really like that. What is to be done with man if we are to help him out of his trouble? This work of helping man by the power of God is what we mean by the word "salvation." This was illustrated in the Bible in the case of the Hebrews when they were in Egypt.

The Hebrews in the land of Egypt were in real trouble.

They did not belong there; they were aliens. Others saw them multiply and envied them. They were hated because there were so many of them, and they were capable and powerful. They were abused and persecuted by the Egyptians, who invoked certain laws against them and made them laborers under duress so that they were actually being used to build big public buildings for the Egyptians. This trouble could not be changed or removed in the land of Egypt.

Moses, recognizing the trouble for what it was, tried to remove the trouble by changing both the Egyptians and the Israelites. He undertook to stop the Egyptian from abusing the Hebrew with the result that the Egyptian was killed. The next day he tried to stop the two Hebrews from quarreling with the result they both turned on him. So Moses' first attempt to bring some sort of relief from their trouble was a failure and the way to relief was not shown until forty years later.

The way to relief in the matter of trouble is to get out of it. In other words, when the ship is sinking, what is to be done? The thing to do is to abandon the ship: get out of it. That is the first thing to do, and this was demonstrated in the case of Israel. If Israel was to be blessed of God they must get out of the land of Egypt.

Between the land of Egypt and the land of Canaan there was a wide stretch of country, commonly called the wilderness, sometimes called the desert. Here the Hebrews had trials and tribulations. They were free from Egypt but they were under difficult circumstances. In this condition they were pilgrims. They did not belong in the desert. This would not be their home. God guided them through the desert with a cloud by day and the fire by night. You may wonder why God did not arrange it so that when they got out of Egypt they would immediately be in the land of Canaan.

That is very much like asking why a baby is not born six feet tall, weighing two hundred pounds. Among other things, the baby would not know how to act. A baby needs to be taught. These Hebrews needed to learn the ways of God. On their way they were sustained by manna, fed by

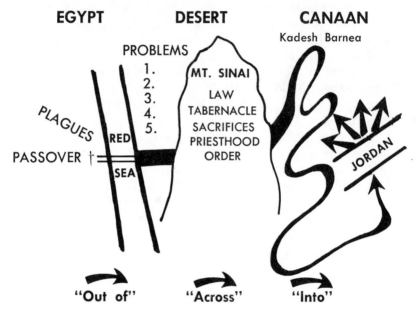

## EGYPT          DESERT          CANAAN

Kadesh Barnea

PROBLEMS

1.
2.
3.
4.
5.

PLAGUES

PASSOVER †

RED
SEA

MT. SINAI

LAW
TABERNACLE
SACRIFICES
PRIESTHOOD
ORDER

JORDAN

"Out of"          "Across"          "Into"

**THE EXODUS:** *"The Course of Events"*

bread from heaven; their thirst was quenched from the rock; all in Providence. When they were in battle with Amalek they were helped to victory through intercessory prayer. With Moses on the mount praying for him, Joshua fought Amalek; then Aaron and Hur helped Moses, turning the tide of victory. The Israelites learned they could be victorious over their enemy who was stronger than they if they called upon God through united intercessory prayer. They then came to Mount Sinai and there they learned by revelation about the law of God. They also learned what to do in case they did wrong; the tabernacle showed them how a sinner could come to God. They also learned at Mount Sinai how they should travel. They were arranged in order: three tribes here, three tribes there, three tribes over yonder, and three tribes back here; the twelve tribes arranged in an orderly fashion which became their standard.

They followed it all the time. As they traveled across the desert, which took them several years, they were finally confronted by a major challenge. They could have gone into Canaan at the end of two years, but they failed because of their unbelief. Here again they learned that just because God had been gracious and had blessed them did not mean that everything was going to come to them regardless of what they did. They found out they must still believe in God and trust Him, but they failed to do that at Kadesh-Barnea. Then a new generation came along, and the third phase of salvation is demonstrated when the Hebrews, the children of Israel, came into the land that was promised to them. This new generation inherited everything from the past but they went on to something new; they entered into the land in obedience to God.

These people were to enter into the land by faith. They were given from God the principle of appropriation. There is a way in which you can have the promises of God fulfilled and it is shown in these words when Joshua was given this promise, "Every place where the sole of your foot shall tread upon shall be yours." In other words, possession of the blessing of God in the fulfillment of God's plan would be possible through obedience. They were to obey Him in the new land. This is the classic pattern of salvation. It was demonstrated in Israel and it is experienced in the case of an individual.

As believers live in this world naturally, they will be in trouble. The Lord Jesus said, "In the world you shall have tribulation but be of good cheer, I have overcome the world." They will be in trouble, but they can come out of trouble. They will pass through trials after which they will come into rest by believing in God through obedience to Him. The believer is to put the sole of his foot upon the promise of God, and, walking upon the promises of God, he will be received into His presence with joy. This again is the classic pattern of salvation demonstrated in what happened to the children of Israel during the Exodus.

## Chapter 10

## SALVATION WAS REALIZED THROUGH
## A SAVIOR

Have you ever understood how important it was that God sent His servant as a man to work out salvation for men?

It is very important that we realize that salvation is the work of God through Christ. I want to draw your attention to a very common error. It is a common mistake to think that salvation, being blessed of God, is the consequence of something we do. If a man were to work for his own salvation so that he would be the one who is responsible for his being blessed of God, then it would be a fitting thing to teach him the principles that he should employ. They should be talked about. Time should be given to describing the activities that he should practice. If I were to be involved, you should describe the ways in which I should proceed that I might achieve the blessing of God. In fact, all of this could be presented as a community project, and we could hear again the words, "Let us make us brick and let us build us a city." This is what the men in Babel did, but it is not the way of salvation.

This "self-salvation" is not a little matter; it is diametrically opposed to the truth. It is entirely different. This is as if I were trying to get across a lake either by rowing in a rowboat or by having an outboard motor put on that boat, so that I could sit back and let the motor take me over. The difference I have in mind is like the difference in climbing the stairs to get to the tenth floor, and stepping into an elevator and being lifted to the tenth floor. You can't do both. Yet there are many people, in their attempt to qualify for the blessing of God, who would have you think that a person should trust God and then go out and work for his blessing.

The very name "Jesus" — the Greek word "Jesus" — is a contraction of the Hebrew phrase "Jehovah is my Savior." Salvation takes place when one person believes in the one Lord who is our Lord Jesus Christ, Almighty God the Father, and the Holy Spirit. All of the issues of eternity, of heaven and hell, take place in the single heart. All those issues take place in my heart.

When God created man, He made him one. He made one man and one woman, and they twain became one flesh. That is the way it started. When God revealed His saving power in response to faith, he used one man, Abraham. Through him, He offered salvation to the whole world. When God demonstrated His plan of salvation in Israel it is true many people were saved, but through one leader, Moses. I am emphasizing the fact that in working with man, God works through one person. Moses was a man sent from God. When Moses died, God set up Joshua as one man. Of course, there was the whole nation, but one man would lead. When God brought victory and peace to the children of Israel He would work through one man, the judge. In Gideon's time it was Gideon. In Samson's time it was Samson. When God revealed His kingdom it is true the kingdom involved many people but the kingdom was all headed up in one person, one king, David.

When God became incarnate, when He came into this world to redeem, He came into this world as one man who was to be offered as a sacrifice. He did not come as a nation. He did not come as a group. He came as one man. When God prepared a sacrifice to substitute for us, He prepared the Lamb of God, one person. When God offered Himself for us He was one person on the cross. I am sure there are many people who have died for various reasons but there was only one Calvary, only one person on the cross. That day three people died on the cross but it was the one in the center that we think about. When God planned a new life for the believer, and He had in mind that the person who would believe in Him would be given the newness of life, He had one person raised from the dead: Jesus of Nazareth.

If all that is given to man for his salvation is a description of the end result, what he is to look like or if all that is given to anybody is an analysis of the principles that would produce a blessed character, or if all that is given to a person in seeking to win him to the Lord is an exhortation that he should avoid evil and endorse virtue, then the whole thrust of my teaching and preaching would be to achieve blessing by works. But that would not be the Bible or the way of truth. If I am going to be saved it is because of my particular personal faith in one person, Jesus Christ. It is when I put my trust in Jesus Christ that Almighty God will save my soul.

Every now and again one hears this criticism of the Gospel: that when we state it that way we make it too simple. I wonder if it can be too simple. I wonder if that is a valid criticism. I don't want to be too somber in talking to you just now, but so far as death is concerned, it takes place in one person. You may say a thousand people were drowned in a certain tidal wave that swept through a coastal city, and that may be true; but no one person was drowned a thousand times. Each person was drowned once. This is very important. I want you to realize that when we talk about the promises of God that are in Christ Jesus, they are for you. As long as I feel I am one of a group I can hope to slip by without being noticed. If I am going as one of a group I go along with the bunch. It doesn't make much difference what I think. That is not the way you come to Christ. Believers come one at a time. It is always one person believing in one Lord for salvation.

You will remember how the Lord Jesus illustrated the whole plan of salvation in the Lord's Supper: "Take, eat; this is my body." And who eats? One person. You may say there may be several hundred people ir church who partook communion. Yes, you can describe it in a general way like that but several hundred people don't eat a piece of bread. Each person eats a piece of bread.

Salvation is made possible because we put our trust in

another single person like ourselves. I am saved through another person like me: the one and only Lord Jesus Christ, my Savior.

*Chapter 11*

## ISRAEL IN EGYPT

Have you ever considered that each human being starts living in this world in trouble? And it is only in the Gospel of Jesus Christ that whosoever believeth in Him shall arrive at peace.

Everybody wants rest and peace, but no one ever has it at the beginning. That is something that we need to take note of at the very outset. The story of our lives is not a matter of everything starting out sweetly, of our doing wrong and having things go sour, and then working back to where all is sweet again. We started out in trouble.

In this study we are interested in salvation, which is the work of God that brings peace to the human heart. The revelation of God's plan of salvation and how He will bring that to pass is given in Scripture. The promise of blessing was given to Abraham because he believed God. Abraham believed God and it was counted to him for righteousness. That promise was renewed to Isaac and to Jacob, who became Israel, and it applied to all his seed. So we have in the Bible the record of this family: Abraham and Isaac, then Jacob, then all his seed, called the children of Israel, who have become the people of God. The children of Israel can then be taken from Scripture as being the people of God.

Many persons have wondered about calling the people of Israel "the chosen people." Often it has been assumed this meant that they were something special, that they were better than other people and different; and thus they were chosen in the sense they were given special privilege. But this is actually human thinking and is not true to the Bible story. The Bible would say that Abraham was chosen to be an example, and that Israel was also chosen to be an example. It is as if I were teaching a class and wanted to demonstrate something by illustration. I might take one boy and bring him up in front of the class and with him I would demonstrate by his actions what I meant. This does not make that boy better than anybody else, and when the time comes for examination he would have to pass his courses just like everybody else. But he was my choice to demonstrate what I had in mind. The children of Israel were chosen to demonstrate what God had in mind about blessing people. The Bible records the experiences of Israel to show the plan of God to bring His favor to mankind, to all men everywhere.

The first major event in the history of Israel was the Exodus of Israel out of Egypt across the wilderness into the land of Canaan. This is a pattern of the work of salva-

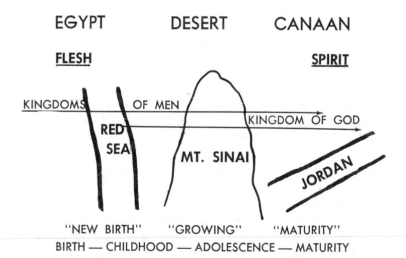

## THE PLAN OF SALVATION: SPIRITUAL SIGNIFICANCE

tion. There are some very simple elements in this whole event. The children of Israel started in this whole program in Egypt where they did not belong. Then they went on a pilgrimage through the wilderness where they were not going to stay. After this they entered into the promised land which had been prepared for them, where they would find rest and peace.

That history is meaningful to us and in that outline we can see the plan of salvation. This situation becomes meaningful to us when we see that Egypt can be considered as this world, the natural world. The Hebrews were there as foreigners, aliens. That is what the word "Hebrew" means. The word "Hebrew" comes from a basic Hebrew word "Heber," which means "over the hill," "from over yonder." In our common idiom we say about someone who comes into our community as a newcomer, that he came in "over the hill," and everybody would understand that means from some faraway place; he is an immigrant. Because he is an alien he does not really belong here. It is easy to be suspicious of him, and often such a person is abused by society as a whole. So it was with the children of Israel. They became slaves in bondage and in distress.

The people of God today, like the children of Israel in their case, are strangers in this world, living *in* this world, it is true, but not *of* this world, to be sure. You will read in the seventeenth chapter of John's Gospel that the Lord Jesus makes it plain, "I have chosen them out of the world. They are in the world but not of the world." And Paul, talking about this says, "Our citizenship is in heaven." That is where believers belong. They are like Americans in a country like France or Russia; their citizenship is in the United States but they are visiting or staying temporarily in other places.

Paul could say, "Our citizenship (where we really belong) is in heaven." It is important to keep one thing in mind: the child of God does not belong here. It is a big temptation to accept this world as ours and to build our hopes here, but it is not our world. We do not belong here, and the very fact that we do not belong here causes some people in this world to be suspicious of us, to envy and to hate us because we are strangers to them. We are pilgrims.

It is true if we have any money it belongs here. If we take part in any amusement, it belongs here. If we share in any entertainment, it belongs here. And if we have privileges among people in society, all such things belong here. They are not in the Gospel. The Gospel, telling us about Jesus Christ, comes as good news from a far country and is the beginning of our relief. We can be free from this world. Even the experiences of human love that we have — our homes, our families — belong here. Because they belong here any one of them can be blemished and can have distress and disaster. Even happiness belongs here and it is something we have for the moment in this place.

All these things are here in this world. We will be noticing, as we study along in this matter of salvation, that God brings blessing to His people not here but in the heavenly places, in spiritual things. Let me remind myself over and over that the blessing of God does not mean that I am going to be favored or fortunate or rich so far as this world is concerned. I may have riches here and I may be blessed here, but this is not where I belong. This is not where I am going to stay; and no matter how much I may be able to get hold of here, I can't take it with me.

The most important thing for us as believing people to realize is the simple fact that so far as this world is concerned, we do not own this place. It is not ours. We are going to leave it. We don't belong here.

## Chapter 12

## ISRAEL UNDER GOD

Do you realize that a believer serves God not in order to win a place with Him but because he already has a place with Him?

Much of life as we live it is already settled even before we get here. I did not have a thing to do with who my parents were, however important that is, and whatever it may be that my family may contribute to me or take away from me. That was not my business. I did not make the language that I speak, but I learned it and I use it. I did not make the times in which I live as they are. I did not arrange for many things that I will have to face.

In the affairs of this world much was already settled before I was born; and this is true, also in spiritual matters. Let us consider the realities in the spiritual world. God is. That is not because I thought it would be a good idea to have a God. He is in Himself as He is. Heaven is not because I agree to it; it actually is as it is. Christ Jesus has already come. It isn't a matter of my thinking it would be a fine thing if we had a Savior. He has come, He has died, He has risen from the dead. All that is settled. It is not an issue whether or not resurrection would be a good idea nor whether it is possible. The resurrection had already taken place before I came on the scene. Christ Jesus has ascended into heaven; He went up in full view of all and He is coming again. And that is exactly the way I believe it. "This same Jesus shall so return in like manner as you have seen Him go." There is nothing I can do to change any part of the spiritual world. So far as the spiritual world is concerned, God is in the very center of it.

Even if I am in trouble down here, if I am in distress,

God is on the throne. If I say, "I don't like what He is doing," that will not make one bit of difference. And if I say,
"I don't think it is like that," even that won't make any
difference. The truth of the matter is "Thou, God, seest
me." Then so far as my life is concerned, as things happen,
regardless of how they seem to be or how they look, the
Bible has a word about that: "He doeth all things well."
God holds all things in the hollow of His hand and God
watches over His own.

As we study what was revealed in the case of the children of Israel in the land of Egypt, it will be helpful if
we can think of the children of Israel in the land of Egypt
as similar to the people of God today in this world. We
should remember Egypt is real, just as the natural world
is really so. God has permitted it to be that way. As ugly
as it is, as hurtful as it is, exactly the way the situation is
in this world, Almighty God has permitted it. Oppression
was hard for Israel. God allowed that. In the world today
there is trouble. God allows that. Some of us have physical
affliction. God allows that. If we want to do the will of
God we should remember He sees all and He knows exactly
what happens when the innocent person is hurt, when the
honest man is lied to. I may feel I am helpless in this
world. God knows that, too. I cannot manage things. God
knows that, and holds all in His own hand. I may feel distressed, downhearted, and frightened about the future, but
God sees and is watching over the whole thing. At times
we may feel like crying out, "Couldn't God do something
about it?" Yes, He could do something about it; and let me
tell you very firmly, He *has* done something about it.

The big thing you and I can have in mind is that He sent
His only begotten Son into this world to do something
about it. Long before anyone should close the book with
a judgment against God for being harsh and cruel, he should
remember this: He sent His own Son right into this world
to suffer with us. God's people are crying in this world.
But you can be sure He hears them. God's people are
praying, and He hears them. We must understand that
God will do what is necessary that His people might be
redeemed, that His people might be delivered. We may be

confused at times because the fulfillment of the promises of God is not always to be seen. God does not always promise us open success, but God knows and He cares.

We are reminded of the way it was with the apostle Peter when the Lord Jesus told the disciples what would happen to Him and to them, how He would be taken to the cross and put to death. We recall how Peter spoke up about it, feeling something should be done. The Lord Jesus then uttered these remarkable words: "What I do thou knowest not now. Thou shalt know hereafter." Insofar as the children of Israel are concerned, in all their trouble God was on the throne; He heard every cry and when the time came for God to move, He moved. He delivered them.

God is not going to fail. He is going to work out His purposes. When the Israelites was under God, they were blessed. When we live our lives under God, recognizing, trusting, and looking to God, we, too, can be blessed.

## Chapter 13

## MOSES SENT FROM GOD

Can you understand that it is the kindness and the grace of God that prompts Him to send a messenger to the children of men?

Salvation as the work of God can operate only in the soul of the believer. A soul can believe only when it hears, when it understands. If it does not hear, it cannot believe. It understands only when the message which it hears is put in human terms. Paul said, "The natural man receiveth not the things of the Spirit of God for they are foolishness unto him, neither can he know them because they are spiritually discerned," and so the Gospel has to be translated out of the spiritual into the natural world's language.

God employs messengers: persons who know Him and also know people, and are the go-betweens. Peter describes them when he says, "Holy men of God spake as they were moved by the Holy Ghost." Being moved by the Holy Ghost was spiritual, but the way these men spoke was in the language of the people. These are the men who have developed a communion with God personally, so they can receive spiritually the will of God. They first come to know the Word of God, and then, because they are men, they communicate this to men. What they have learned is the will of God but when they express it to people it comes out in practical events and in natural things in this world's affairs.

One can think of a situation that would exist in any family. The mother may know deep down in her heart very well what God would want the child to do, so the mother tells the child to do it. The child does not recognize the message as the Word of God; the child recognizes only the mother and reacts to the mother. Many times the Word of God as it is felt in the heart of the parent and is communicated to the child seems to the child to be an overbearing attitude on the part of the father and mother. The child may feel that is not the thing to do; however, the parent knows that is the will of God that this should be done.

We see this in the case of Israel when we consider the man Moses, who was sent from God to perform a task of leadership with the people. Moses was to be in the presence of God where he would learn what God wanted. Then he would tell the people what the will of God was. In Deuteronomy 5:23-28 the procedure is described in just that way. It appears that God agreed, as it were, to that arrangement. The people asked Moses to talk to God because they were afraid He might destroy them because of their sinfulness. Moses agreed to go into the presence of God to learn His will for them. In the course of his life Moses demonstrated the providence of God.

If you were to look for a messenger to come to you to tell you the Word of God, the thought might occur to you that if that messenger were an angel or someone extraordinary, you could be impressed with that. One of the biggest problems we have when we teach the Word of God as the will of God to people is that the people say it does not apply to them. And this is why God has those who live among the people in this world tell them the Word of God. Often those of us who preach and are sincere in our hearts are conscious of our own infirmities and shortcomings so that we feel almost apologetic when we preach. We ourselves could sometimes wonder why God does not send an angel, like Gabriel, to preach. It is easy to misunderstand the providence of God when we see in preachers human weakness. We may even feel inclined to make a big "to do" about it, and under certain circumstances some people will even gossip about it. But right here is an amazing truth! The marvelous thing about the Gospel is that it is sinners who are saved and it is they who can tell it. It is possible that the human weakness in a preacher is there so that people will understand that the man talking to them is a human being like themselves. He is not an angel; he is one being led of the Lord to do certain things, just as they could be led.

I think of some parents who may have a terrible feeling that if they were just the kind of person they ought to be, their children would turn out to be perfect. Wait a minute! God is the kind of being He ought to be, and they don't even turn out all right for Him; so parents should not take it too much to heart if their children do not turn out all right for them. It may be that for the time being they can even share in the grief and in the sorrow that God Himself feels because He made them. Let us have in mind that when the parent is just a human being with human foibles and peculiarities, on occasion showing human limitations, such a person could be the most effective messenger for the Gospel, because that person could actually say "Christ saved me; Christ forgave me."

With reference to Moses, it can be remembered that often under the responsibility of leadership a man will do better than he could do any other way. Just so, often under the responsibility of leadership a woman will do better. I don't question at all that a mother is at her best when she is actually in a home situation as mother, because then she has to think of someone else; this gets very close to what we have in the Gospel. Moses' life was marked by the providence of God. He did not choose to come into this world. He did not choose his characteristics so that he would be this or that kind of person. That was God's business. The fact that his parents were godly believers was God's business, the fact that he was adopted by Pharaoh's daughter, the fact that his sister Miriam was there to suggest to Pharaoh's daughter that she knew a nurse who would take care of the baby, so that his mother came to do it, was all God's business.

Being adopted into the household of Pharaoh was a great advantage to Moses. We begin to understand why it was said about him that Moses was learned in all the wisdom of the Egyptians. God arranged that.

In the course of Moses' life several great things happened that we shall be noting; one that I want to note just now is the great act on the part of Moses when he renounced the possibilities that were ahead of him:

> By faith Moses, when he was born, was hid three months of his parents, because they saw he was a proper child; and they were not afraid of the king's commandment. By faith Moses, when he was come to years, refused to be called the son of Pharaoh's daughter; choosing rather to suffer affliction with the people of God, than to enjoy the pleasures of sin for a season; esteeming the reproach of Christ greater riches than the treasures in Egypt: for he had respect unto the recompence of the reward (Heb. 11:23-26).

In this record we see that Moses, when he was old enough to make his choice, refused to take advantage of his position in Pharaoh's household where he might have eventually become Pharaoh, and chose to suffer affliction with his own people.

The whole idea of Moses leading the people out of Egypt did not arise out of Moses' own heart or spirit. This was God's idea. The work of salvation may involve the participation of chosen servants who are sent to preach and to teach a project not of their own making. I suspect we could say with reference to that, so far as we as parents are concerned, when young people get married and begin a family, they hardly ask for the responsibility of teaching that child the ways of the Lord but that is what they have to do. The witnesses who tell the Gospel, whether at home, in the community, in the pulpit, or in the mission field, are sent from God.

## Chapter 14

## FIRST ATTEMPT A FAILURE

Do you realize that even if a person does not know how to witness effectively and is unsuccessful, he may still be the man to do it?

At this point we can notice a very important truth about salvation. We understand that salvation is the work of God, but we have noted that He uses human agents. Now we shall see that just because a person is committed to serving God and is sincere, this is no guarantee that he will know how to do it. Whenever we think about this matter of spreading the Gospel and of teaching people about the Gospel, we sometimes wonder why God didn't send perfect people to do it, or why He did not give the message to the angels; but He did not: He called folks like you and me to be His witnesses for a very simple reason that is right on the surface. Every time a sinner who has been brought to the Lord Jesus Christ opens his mouth to talk, he is a living demonstration of the fact that God will deal with a man like that. This is one reason why the important thing about the witness is that he should know personally that he does belong to God in spite of anything and everything he may have been or may not have been, or may not have done. Because God called him, he belongs to Him and he can now stand up and tell the whole world "whosoever will may come." If one wanted proof he could say, "Look at me. I came and here I am."

Even though a witness is a true servant of Christ he may fail at some point. And even though he fails on occasion, he may yet be the very person who is to carry that task on to completion. As I write this I think of parents, and even of myself as a parent. I remember the days when my children were young and I was doing the best I could to show them the way to go and how to do things; I often wished that they had a father who could really teach them something and really show them something. I felt personally unfit to be the one who would show them what was right and what was wrong, and who would insist that they do what was right, when deep down in my own heart I realized that I myself was one who had not always done right. In spite of this humbling fact, even though it may be true that those of us who witness may on occasion fail and at some point go about our tasks in the wrong way, yet we may be the very persons who are to carry that witnessing through to its completion, in the plan of God.

All this is demonstrated in the case of Moses, chosen of God for a great service. He was to lead the people of God out of Egypt across the wilderness into the land of Canaan, a tremendous task, making him one of the outstanding leaders of all history. This one man was responsible for changing the circumstances and the culture of an entire nation in one generation.

He responded to the call of God when he was forty years of age. He made the big choice, the great renunciation so far as he was concerned, yet Moses had been a failure in his first attempt. When Moses went out to see how his brethren were getting along, he saw an Egyptian abusing a Hebrew. He interfered, and in his attempt to stop that injustice the Egyptian was killed. The next day he saw two Hebrews quarreling and he told them, "You are brothers, you shouldn't quarrel." They turned on him and said, "Who made you a ruler and a judge? Are you going to kill us the way you killed the Egyptian yesterday?" Moses knew then that his act of violence was known and that he had to flee for his life. That was his first attempt.

As we think about this event, let us consider several things. Moses' heart was right. He had turned away from all the privileges he could have had in Pharaoh's household, and had committed himself to walk with those Hebrews who were slaves. There was injustice and he saw it. Something, he felt, ought to be done about that. Then he saw there was contention among the Hebrews, and he felt that ought not to happen. But Moses' understanding of how to proceed was mistaken. He was in no way deceitful about his actions. He just simply did not know how to do things. He was ignorant at that point of God's way of doing what needed to be done. This is a clear illustration that sincerity will not compensate for ignorance. It really does not matter how much you may want to do something, if you do not know how to do it you will fail. It may seem that this observation gives to technique in procedure a very prominent place; but is true. It is a fact that if you want to raise beans you will have to plant them in the ground at a certain time of the year and at a certain depth. You could not put them six feet under and get beans; and you could not leave them on the top of the ground and get beans. You must plant them as beans are supposed to be planted. No matter how sincere you may be, this is still the way it is about beans.

As a young lad I lived on the farm, and often worked with my father, who was a successful farmer. In our neighborhood we sometimes saw very fine men who raised very poor crops. This was generally because they did not know what to do. Moses' attempt to do what he thought was necessary and what seemed to him to be the important thing failed because he went at it in the wrong way.

I am going through this discussion slowly because I am thinking of those who are parents. I do not want to make any parent feel bad, but I do want each one to be really honest about this whole matter. A parent may wonder why his child did not turn out right, when it seems to him that he did everything he should have done. But wait a minute! How would the parent know he had done everything as he should have? He may be satisfied he did everything he thought was right. But that may not be the case! If a person goes about a task in the wrong way, he will actually have poor results or no results at all. This may not be true in every case. But there may be some parent right now whose heart is hurting because his child has not done the right thing. Any parent should remember if he seems to have failed in dealing with his child, that God failed, too. God started with that person, He made that person, and He did not want that person to do wrong; but it sometimes happens!

As we look at Moses we see the right man with a true awareness of the actual need, the real true situation, in attempting to correct what was wrong in his own way, failed. There was violence and rejection. This does not mean that he was the wrong man on the wrong mission. No, as a matter of fact he was the right man and he meant to do the right thing. What happened showed that because his procedure was wrong, his results also were wrong. This does not mean that he was mistaken in his analysis; he saw the truth. It means only that he was mistaken in his method. A parent may see clearly and yet fail because of the wrong method. A preacher may have the burden but may not know how and he will fail.

This, then, is an important lesson for all of us: the right man doing the right thing must be wise to do it the right way.

*Chapter 15*

## CALL OF MOSES

Do you know that a person who believes in God may be called of God to do something he never expected to do?

It is very common for a person to plan his own program day in and day out as if it were his privilege to choose just what he is going to do, when he is going to do it, and with whom he will do it. It is as if he felt it was all in his own hands so that he could lay it out whatever way he chose. But living does not work out that way; living is filled with surprises.

A person easily forgets that if he could have done as he had planned to do and wanted to do, he would have been in disaster many times. Then again it is just as easy for him to forget that some of the best things that ever happened to him came to pass when he had to do things he never intended to do. How often a person misses some good opportunity which would bring him blessing because he had not intended to do that, because it was not in his plan or he had not thought of it!

In our last study we took note of a very distressing experience in the life of Moses. His first attempt to help his people resulted in failure because, it was noted, the right person with good insight and understanding but following the wrong method will come to failure. I used the illustration of a person trying to raise beans in a garden. There is a more sobering thought: you and I have something far more important to do than raising beans. Some of us have children of our own, some of us have relatives and friends. We have neighbors. Right away the thought may come that we are not getting along with a neighbor or not succeeding in winning a relative of ours. Is it possible that there is something about the way we are going about it? That could be. That could also be true with a wife and her husband.

Peter tells us something about that. What Peter has to say is along the line that the wife should not talk so much and that she should not tell the husband what to do. This is found in I Peter 3:1-2. This principle is true in all relationships. It is true in what happens between a parent and his child. Any father or mother in his or her right mind really wants to help the children. Parents mean to do this but the truth is they could go about it in the wrong way and thus defeat the very purpose they have in mind.

Sometimes we can see people dealing with others, such as parents dealing with children, and it seems they are standing in their own light. They are defeating their own purpose. I realize this is a very sobering line of thought but it is important to be honest and sincere when we have something important to say.

Let us turn to Moses again. When we think about the fact that Moses failed we could think, "That must have shaken him up." But that was not the most sobering thing for Moses. The most sobering thing was the consequence: Moses had to flee. He spent forty years in the desert. It would be easy to miss what was involved in that. Having spent the first forty years of his life in Pharaoh's household, tradition has it that Moses became a great military leader. We may be sure he learned a great deal because the Bible tells us he was "learned in all the wisdom of the Egyptians." By the time one third of his life had passed there need be no doubt that Moses was well educated and well trained in many different ways. It is doubtful that many stirring experiences occurred during the forty years Moses lived in the desert.

There is no record to give any clue as to his personal thoughts during that period. This absence of a record speaks to me. It tells me that his personal thoughts and his personal impressions did not matter; they really did not have any bearing on the outcome. During his time in the desert Moses married and had two sons. When he was eighty there was a day when he saw a bush burning that was not consumed. A bush on fire that was not being burned up was a strange thing. We can understand how it happened that Moses said, "I will turn aside now and see this strange sight." When he did, God spoke to him.

"Put off thy shoes from off thy feet, for the place whereon thou standeth is holy ground" (Exod. 3:5). God intended to deal with Moses. God was going to give him a commission. Moses did not have to go anywhere. God did not say, "If you move over here you may get it," or "If you were back over here, you could get it." The call of God will come to you right where you are. You will not have to move. You have only to recognize right now that you are in the presence of God. This is where it starts. Then God goes on, "I have surely seen the affliction of my people which are in Egypt. I will send thee that thou mayest bring them out of Egypt."

When we read that from this distance it is hard to realize just what it really meant. We know that Moses was a great man, and he became a wonderful leader. But for forty years this man had been a shepherd with no contact with his home country at all. His last effort to help his people had been a failure, and since then he had made a life for himself. Now God comes to say, "I am going to send you and you are to bring them out." It is no wonder Moses' response is "Who am I? Why pick on me?" No doubt Moses was concerned because he had failed before. His question shows that he is still thinking in terms of that failure. But Moses is to learn God will do it. He assures Moses, "Certainly I will be with them."

This is the big thing in God's plan. The deliverance will be led by Moses, and God will be with him. I would like to say to every one of you if you are a father or a mother, "Father, it will be you and God; Mother, it will be you and God. Do not take it all on yourself. It is not supposed to depend all on yourself. All you are to be is faithful to your commission. Certainly God will be with you."

Moses asked a very practical question. "When they shall say, 'What is His name, this Person Who is with you?'" Then God told him this strange name that we hear about all through the Bible but we never can fully grasp. "I am that I am." Then He said, "Thus shalt thou say unto the children of Israel, I am hath sent me unto you." When the Lord Jesus Himself was speaking about these things and people asked Him, "Are you greater than Abraham?" He answered and said, "Before Abraham was, I am." He is saying to Moses, "Just tell them that the great Almighty God their Creator and their Keeper is with you."

The call came to Moses unexpectedly, while he was in his routine place doing the things he ought to do. And your call could come to you while you are in your kitchen or while you are in your office. God could be saying to you, "I am going to be with you when you deal with that child. I am going to be with you when you live in that home. I am going to be with you when you are working in that church." The natural skepticism that Moses felt in his own heart was met by God's act. The sovereign act of Almighty God was that He would use Moses to accomplish His purpose.

## Chapter 16

## PROBLEM OF MOTIVATION

Has it ever occurred to you that no one will ever be saved unless he wants to be?

"When Jesus saw him (a lame man) lie, and knew that he had been now a long time in that case, he saith unto him, Wilt thou be made whole?" (John 5:6). Notice the simple way in which it was stated. When Jesus saw this lame man beside the pool of Bethesda and knew that he had been now a long time in that case, He said to him, "Wilt thou be made whole?" Do you want to be cured?

Salvation is the work of God. This we realize and keep in mind. It is God who does it. But this action of God is not arbitrary; by that we mean this work of God is not forced on anybody. No one will ever be forced into heaven. God looks upon the heart. He knows what men want. He looks for willing hearts. Those who will do His will are those who are acceptable. Salvation begins by a call from God. That call from God is sometimes in words, but often it is not. Sometimes it is only some words and a good deal of action, but always there is the challenge in "Come." "Come to the Savior, make no delay. Here in our midst, He is standing today, tenderly saying, Come."

John reports that the Lord Jesus said, "If any man will do his will, he shall know of the doctrine" (John 7:17). In other words, God is looking for the person with a willing heart. We are studying this in the case of the Hebrews — Israel in Egypt. God was going to bring the Israelites out of Egypt by His grace and by His power; but the Israelites must be willing to come, and this willingness will be seen in their obedience to the call. We are going to see that

Pharaoh needed to be willing that they should leave. This was also a problem.

When we say that God is looking for the willinghearted, we ask ourselves a simple question: willing to do what? We mean willing to leave the old, the familiar, the natural — everything I have in myself. The call came to Abraham, "Come out from thy country from thy father's house. Come out." And the Lord Jesus, in speaking about that, on one occasion said, "If any man loves father or mother more than he loves me, he is not worthy of me." Actually we must be willing to leave self, everything that has to do with self. All of my human circumstances, my human resources and values — whatever they are — I must be willing to leave. I must be willing to trust God in the present. I do not know everything. I can't see everything. I do not know why things are as they are. I did not make them that way. It is not my responsibility, and I do not know how they are going to be. I do not know what the future will be. Even as things are right now, I do not know what is going to happen to me. So what? So I must be willing to trust God at present and I will depend on God for the future. No man knows what a day will bring forth. How can any man come to God with quietness and confidence and the future all unknown? By trusting God. There is no other way to be happy in Jesus but to trust and obey.

The issue of trusting in God can be felt at all times, but it shows up most clearly at the very first of the salvation experience, when the call is to come out of the old into the ways of God. Let us look at the people of Israel as they were in Egypt and try to understand how the problem actually developed there. The children of Israel had been in the land of Egypt four hundred years. They were, as we would say, accommodated to living there. They may not have liked everything about it but it was home to them. And man does not like to change. This is a basic principle in human nature. It is very natural that a child does not want to go to bed at night, very natural that he does not want to get up in time for school in the morning. Inertia is natural. It is a kind of personal and psychological, if not almost moral, inertia. I want to keep on going the way

I am going, because where I am and where I have been the attachments are very real. I have plans. I have in myself a certain resistance to change. I do not want to be different.

After all, I do not know what is going to happen tomorrow. If you are going to take me out over a new road I have the fear of the unknown. The attachments I have to where I live, the resistance I have to any kind of change at all, and the fear I have for the future are enough to keep me right where I am. The whole problem of getting me to want to be different is God's problem in providence, and He has a way of going about it. It is very interesting. He does not lead me away from where I am by promising me something better at first.

The first thing that happened to Israel was that the situation in Egypt became unbearable. Ill will developed among the Egyptians. There were so many of the Hebrews and they were prospering in so many ways that the Egyptians became suspicious of them. When the Egyptians became suspicious, they did not like the Hebrews and began to hate them. When they began to hate them, they began to abuse them. The Hebrews were prosperous. God had blessed them, and the Egyptians became jealous. When there is jealousy there is hatred, and that brings on violence.

Before long there was open conflict and the Egyptians actually abused the Hebrews in various ways. They forced them to do free labor on their big building projects. The Hebrews had to make the brick for these buildings and when they complained about it the Egyptians withheld the straw. They had to collect the straw with which to make the brick. Things were made harder and harder for them. The oppression was very real and the people groaned because of it. Then in the providence of God there came along a leader. Moses came with a program. He proposed to these people, "Let us leave this country and go to the land we are supposed to be in, the land of Canaan." As he talked to them, can you understand how appealing this call would be to these people who were having so much trouble where they were?

This is often the way God will do things. If you have in your family or among your friends someone whom you wish would turn to the Lord, you could start praying that he would turn. If you start praying that the person will turn to the Lord and that person has trouble, don't try to stop it. Don't get in there and start taking the trouble away. That trouble may be God's way of doing it. People often are not willing to move until the situation they are in becomes unbearable; sometimes that is not felt in pushing but just in hurting. Sometimes it is when you find that the very things you cherish can be lost. You may have a precious treasure which you may lose, something in your home may be broken, your lovely home may be burned, your close friend may die, you may have labor troubles in your shop, you may have competition and people may misrepresent you, and folks may get you into trouble. These things may add up to the point that you are sick and tired of the whole business, and God may let these things happen. But you can put your whole trust in Him.

This is one of the ways God has of moving us to be willing to take His way out. Often people will turn to the Lord when they are in real trouble, when they are at the very bottom of their own personal resources, and the call comes to turn to the Lord. I think that so far as they are concerned the feeling may sometimes be, "Anything would be better than this." Don't be too upset by their words; what you want to watch is what they will do. In this whole matter of motivation God will work with the soul to help the person want to be different, willing to be changed, willing to accept the Lord. Pray for it, because God can work it out.

*Chapter 17*

## PROBLEMS OF PERMISSION

Do you realize that no big movement, nothing important, can ever happen among believers without the consent of others?

The way human beings live together works out in such a way that one can see a certain structure of relationships. Each one of us has a certain place in the society in which we live. Some are in charge, some have a higher position of responsibility, and some are just free, but all are under obligation. Nobody ever lives entirely to himself. What that means is this that anything I want to do must be done with respect to other people, even if it is only to drive a car. When I go out on the highway to drive, I have the traffic rules to consider. If I am in school I have schedules to keep. If I study in the university I have a course program to study. Even in the family there are certain things for each of us to do in order to get along together. Some agreement must always be reached.

I must receive certain permission from other people if I want to act in a certain way; there is always a problem if I want to change my life style. Suppose I have never gone to prayer meeting and I want to start. Do you realize that will make it necessary for some others to change their ways? Wherever I have lived some people have lived with me. They do not want me to change. If I have been in that frame of mind where I did not go to church, people living with me have become accustomed to it. They may agree I could well be different, but they are not ready for me to be different. Suppose some Sunday I say, "I want to go to church." That would be a shock if I never have. Then again, suppose I say on a certain night when I come home from the office, "Tonight I want to go to prayer meeting." If I have not done that before, such an announcement will be a shock. Suppose there is a church meeting on Friday night where the Bible is being studied, and some man says to his family, "I want to go to the Bible study tonight." If he never has done that, it will create a big stir. A person could probably get permission to do such a thing once, and maybe twice, but do you realize that others would not want him to make a habit of it? They do not want him to be that much different.

As a pastor I worked at different times with people, trying to get them to change their ways. I wanted them to start studying the Bible, I wanted them to start praying, and I encouraged them to give. I learned that many times the biggest problem a man had was right in his own family. Others were not ready for him to change his ways. I can remember such instances as this: a wife who was in great distress because her husband was careless about the church talked to me about it; I suggested we pray about it. The man started coming to church and he went at it whole-heartedly. He came Wednesday night and twice on Sunday. Before long his wife came to me asking what she could do because her husband was spending too much time in church! Unconsciously she wanted him to be different but just a little different. A person who has played a certain part in home or society is expected to keep on doing that, and any attempt to change that way of doing things will meet with opposition.

Now let us look again at the case of the people of Israel in Egypt and see this principle worked out there. God heard their cry and sent a deliverer. Moses came. Moses proposed that the Hebrews leave Egypt. When he went to Pharaoh and asked for permission to leave the country, Pharaoh refused. Pharaoh could abuse these people; he could take advantage of them. They were, after all, an asset to the community. They did a lot of work. Moses was now faced with a complicated problem. Pharaoh needed to become willing to permit these people to leave; we learn it was the plagues that made him willing.

Can we see what that problem would be if it came up

today? Any proposal to change the ways of people must be permitted by other people. For example, if a family has not been going to church or Sunday school at all, and if you want to take their children to Sunday school, do you realize that you are really not free to ask them without first going to their parents and getting permission? Do you realize that if you start taking those children to Sunday school you will be creating a situation in the home where the children are going to be in trouble?

Consider the matter of distributing tracts. There are some people who have a feeling in their hearts that they want to share the news of the Gospel with others by handing out tracts. As a matter of fact when tracts are handed out on buses or even on the street, many people resent it. In fact, in many cities there are laws against it. Suppose that in a congregation an enthusiastic preacher wants to get the people stirred up for doing more for the Lord. He proposes additional meetings in the congregation. He proposes a Sunday evening preaching service. Do you know that today there are many churches in the land with preachers who would be willing to preach on Sunday night but the church officers will not permit them? Why would they do this? I am afraid I can't tell you the whole reason but I could think, among other reasons, they don't want to be made to look bad. If there are church services at the church and some elder is not present it will make him feel that he looks bad. If there is no service at all, he does not have to go; so he would rather not have the service. Anybody who has had anything to do with the leadership of a congregation knows that you just do not take the liberty to invite an evangelist and arrange for a week of meetings. You must get the consent of the officers and of the people. Even when you want to talk about the Lord to people in the community, do you realize that ordinarily others resent it? They do not want you to do it.

It seems it is always wise that one should be very careful to get permission, to say to people, "I hope you don't mind if we do this, or if we do that." Even in the matter of dealing with one's own family, it is not wise to thrust it at them, at every moment. One should not be continually telling them they should go to church, or they should pray, or read the Bible. There will be times when this can be made very clear; your example will be the best way to show it. Suppose that your church is full and people are coming from a community some miles away. Do you think it would be good to open a branch Sunday school over there? Do you realize that opening a branch Sunday school should be checked with all the other people working in that community, and that failure to do so will bring opposition? It may seem fine to say, "I will work as if nobody else in the world were working," but you will not get very far; you will find that people will resist you because you are assuming and presuming something for which you did not ask permission.

I wonder how many of you realize that if a certain church had a building standing in a certain place in some community and because of a change in the real estate situation it seemed practical to move that building out three or four miles, they would need to get permission not only from the city fathers, but from other church people. It could be considered unfriendly for you to start a new church in the community where there are already people busy. This brings up the whole matter of permission.

These were the problems that were faced by Moses when he was going to lead his people. He wanted permission to lead them out of Egypt on a three-day journey into the wilderness, but Pharaoh resisted him. The plagues caused Pharaoh to be willing. These plagues were acts of God, done in such a way that Israel was influenced and impressed by the demonstration of power to trust Moses, and Pharaoh was influenced to give in to Moses temporarily, long enough for Moses to move. Believers always have such problems, as do all witnesses for salvation.

This is the problem of a wife with her husband. She needs to get permission from him for what she is going to do. So also with a parent and child: the parent needs to get the permission of the child to start telling him what he should do about the Lord. You remember Daniel, when he wanted the privilege of not taking part in some of the activities of the others: he went to the school official and asked him for permission to abstain, rather than acting on his own ideas. Jesus of Nazareth, while He was here in this world, submitted Himself to the laws of the land. He paid taxes to the Roman government and submitted to the authority of the Roman governor because He was living in the community. He was the one who would tell you "Render unto Caesar the things that are Caesar's, and unto God the things that are God's." This problem of permission is very real. We can be sure that God will need to help us in His providence, that we might get permission for what we want to do for Him.

## Chapter 18

### PROBLEM OF COMPROMISE

Did you know that if a person wants to share in the salvation of God he must be absolutely sincere?

There is much confusion in the world of thought among people, with many differing ideas even in matters that have to do with the Gospel of the Lord Jesus Christ. In some respects believers in Christ seem to be harder to deal with than people in the world. There seem to be more different ideas about how to live in faith, yet there is one directive for all men everywhere that all believers will accept: "Ye must be born again." In committing himself to God the believer takes up his cross to follow Christ. It is to be feared there are many to whom such commitment is something you are in favor of, something with which you agree; but anything less than total personal commitment is simply not good enough. This matter of being born again, taking up the cross, following Christ is something not only to be said, but it is something to be done.

We will see this truth again now that we think about the children of Israel coming out of the land of Egypt. We will see that they, in their experience, demonstrated something of what we have to face in total commitment. When Israel was being brought out of Egypt, Moses requested permission from Pharaoh. Pharaoh opposed this request; he did not want them to go. He abused them, but as they were an economic asset, he wanted to keep them. Under pressure of the plagues he finally began to yield, though he made several attempts to compromise.

I want to speak just now of those attempts he made to compromise. We may learn much as we see how he presented these suggestions. The first compromise he offered to Moses was this: if the people insisted on worshiping God, they should do that right there in Egypt. Moses turned that down. He said that would not do because if they sacrificed to their God in the land of Egypt the Egyptians would resent it, and there would be contention and distress. You may remember that the Egyptians were people who worshiped animals, and when the Hebrews worshiped God they sacrificed animals. This practice would immediately cause trouble. Here one can see the whole idea that if you are going to worship God you cannot stay in the ways of the world to do it. Jesus of Nazareth said that if a man were coming to God to pray, he should enter into his closet and shut the door, and then pray to his Father in secret. Now that is a special way of saying it. It is easy to see the truth when it is a matter of going into the house to worship God from a shut room, as it were; but this way is, generally speaking, the way it is to be done.

The actual principle means plainly to say that so far as one's whole conduct is concerned, the person who is going to worship God must do so differently. The true worshiper is to come out from others and be different. He is to act in such a way that would indicate that he feels this is the proper way to worship God. In any case, Moses said it would not be acceptable to worship God in the land, so Pharaoh turned away. More plagues came.

After more plagues had come, Pharaoh again made an offer of compromise. He told Moses to take his people out from the land but "only a little way." His thought was that if they went only a little way it would be easy to bring them back. I am sure we can recognize this kind of suggestion if it were made today. People will say, "I'd like to be a Christian; but I would not have to change, would I?" Some might say you could be a Christian and not change at all. The believer would accept Christ and be the same person he is now. That would be worshiping God "in the land," staying right where you are. Other people might say, "You could accept Christ but you will not need to make any big changes. If you want to go to church and read the Bible and pray, that will be all right; but don't make too much disturbance about it. Go just a little way."

Moses answered this offer of compromise very directly: "It will have to be three days' journey." Many have wondered about that "three days." This period can suggest to your mind the three days the Lord Jesus was in the grave. He was really dead for that time. This could be the way it is to be with true believers: they are to be really dead so far as this world is concerned. When Moses said it would have to be a three-day journey into the Wilderness, Pharaoh turned him down again.

With more trouble coming in the way of plagues, Pharaoh called Moses again and told him to go but "leave the children." Of course, the idea behind that was this: if they left the children behind they would come back. This again is the way the world would have it today. I do not know in how many cases, so far as Christians are concerned, spiritual realities fade out and are really sometimes lost for no other reason than this: parents make room to let their children go the way of the world. The first thing you know the parents will be in there with them. Moses said, "No. Those little children belong to us and when we go, they will go."

So often we should recognize again this very interesting fact: people who do not really want you to serve the Lord become very concerned about the little children. They say, "Don't make the poor little children act the way you do and put adult ideas on their poor little minds. Let them choose what they want to choose so they can be free." The truth about human nature is plain: what they really mean is let the children do as we have always done because that is truly the way we want it. But Moses said, "No, the little children belong to us and when we go they will go."

Pharaoh was again enraged by this insistence on the part of Moses. He turned away and said that now he would not let them go at all. But more plagues came and finally Pharaoh called Moses in and said, "All right, if you want to go, you go. Take the children but leave the cattle. Leave your flocks and herds." We can recognize this right away. "You want to be a Christian? You want to have your children grow up in the atmosphere of faith? All right, but don't let it interfere with your business. So far as your business and your social affairs are concerned, leave those things the way they were." But Moses said, "We can't do that. We need the cattle. We need our business with which to serve the Lord." And now the break came. Although Pharaoh made these four offers to compromise, Moses would not compromise at all. So Pharaoh said unto him, "Get thee from me, take heed to thyself, see my face no more...." There was the only time Moses turned on Pharaoh; he said, "Thou hast spoken well, I will see thy face no more."

Moses was predicting what Pharaoh did not know: that night when the angel of death passed through, Pharaoh would want them to leave. Such result would not be unusual even today. No doubt many parents have this whole problem to face. They seek the best for their children and are often called stubborn. They can be called hardheaded and accused of having a "sixteenth-century" mentality. But it is important for the parents to remember *this is the most crucial battle of all* when you are seeking to make a break so far as the world is concerned. Nothing will do but an absolute break. Total, complete commitment to God is the price of success in believing.

## Chapter 19

## PROBLEM OF CONSENT

Do you realize that the one real issue confronting any person who wants the salvation of God is the matter of consent?

Salvation is the work of God. In the Scriptures we have this word, "Come; for all things are now ready" (Luke 14:17). Not only is it true that God saves the soul but it is also true that He has already done all that is necessary for that salvation. We read, for instance, about a certain man who made a great supper and bade many to come. I want us now to think about what is offered in the Gospel. We say to each other with appreciation the Son of Man has come to seek and to save that which is lost. We say in the Word, "He carries away our sins." What does this mean? This means that Christ our Passover has been sacrificed for us. That is already done. We read in the Word and are encouraged to see, "We shall be reconciled to God." How is that possible? The Lamb has been slain. When we read what the apostle Paul and others say, we find that "I am crucified with Him." Calvary is already done. I am to join Him there. I am "buried with Him in baptism." He has already been in the grave. I am "raised in the newness of life": Christ is already raised alive.

As I have gone over this you may have noticed that all those things that are included in the precious truth of the Gospel are already done. We do not need to sin for Jesus Christ to come. He came. We do not now have any part in putting Him on the cross. They put Him there. We do not now need to wait for Him to be raised from the dead. He was raised from the dead. He is risen. We do not now need to wonder about that tomb in which He was put. We know the tomb is empty and has been for more than 1900 years. These things have been done. "All things are now ready." We can read in the Bible how the Lord Jesus gives us this word: "Behold, I stand at the door and knock." He is ready to come in.

As we are thinking about the children of Israel coming out of the land of Egypt, when they were about to be released, the angel of death was to pass through, and the promise was, "When I see the blood I will pass over you." The blood would already have been shed and then when the angel of death came through and saw the blood they would be spared. They would be set free. All that was necessary had already been done.

One thinks about the Lord Jesus Christ when He met His disciples after the resurrection beside the Sea of Galilee. We read that He was there and had some broiled fish on the fire. You will remember His words: "Come and dine." I wonder how I can say this so that it will linger in our hearts? I am trying to emphasize that everything necessary for our salvation has already been done.

Salvation was so dramatized in the time of Israel there was just one thing needed — to put the blood of the lamb on the doorpost. So far as you and I are concerned, we put the blood of Calvary over our hearts. We do this by faith in the Lord Jesus Christ; all that He has done for us is operative. In I Peter 4:19 we read, "Wherefore let them that suffer according to the will of God commit the keeping of their souls to him in well doing, as unto a faithful Creator." God is faithful. He will keep you. The moment I accept Him, He regenerates me as a new creation. He has everything all set for us. When I come to the Lord Jesus Christ I do not come to be tested to see if I qualify; everything about me is already known. When I come into the presence of God in myself, in my own human nature, I am under condemnation and am facing destruction. All I need to do is to commit myself to the living Lord Jesus Christ and believe in Him, and I will believe in Him by obeying Him, by yielding myself to Him. He regenerates me as a new creation. Paul writes in II Corinthians 5:17 these words: "Therefore if any man be in Christ, he is a new creature."

It is not that he now has a chance to develop into one. No. "If any man be in Christ, he is a new creature: old things are passed away; behold, all things are become new."

Now as this process goes on in the individual these things may be fulfilled day in and day out, week after week, month after month, and year after year. These things may be fulfilled but the situation is already settled. Still the dramatic issue that is before all people outside of Christ is just one thing: Will you at this moment believe? Will you at this moment receive? We are seeing great emphasis in the country at the present time on various types of evangelistic work. These projects for bringing the call of the Gospel directly to the individual and asking for a decision are commendable. They are important. The big thing that a person hearing this Gospel message needs to decide is "Will I do it?" That is why I call this the problem of consent. Do I consent to this? "If any man will be my disciple, let him deny himself, take up his cross and follow me." It is just as simple as that.

Any number of people don't want to give up on themselves. They still like themselves the way they are, or they trust themselves as they are, or they don't have any confidence in God, or they don't have confidence in the Bible. Whatever the explanation it will not change the fact. If the call goes out they either come or they don't. "Whosoever will shall be saved." And whosoever won't, won't be saved. That is the way it is. It all comes down to a simple problem of consent. "Come, buy wine and milk without money and without price." You can have it. Just take it. Come and dine.

## Chapter 20

## PROBLEM OF FINAL RELEASE

Can you understand that at the very beginning of belonging to God there must be a final release from the old nature?

We are talking about salvation. We are interested in coming to understand this great work of God wherein He takes a human being and brings him into His own family to make him a child of God. The natural man born into this world is a child of Adam. He must be born again. When he is, he is a child of God. This is what the Bible teaches and we can talk about it more as we go along. There are people who emphasize the fact that God is good to everybody. This is true. He *is* good to everybody if you are willing to include in goodness that death, disease, and suffering will come. In spite of that, God still is good, but that is not the basis of salvation.

When we talk about salvation we are talking about the grace of God, that God extends this grace to those who are willing to believe, those who receive Christ Jesus as their Savior. When Christ Jesus is working in you, you then share in the salvation work of God. No doubt there are many people seeking the blessing of God in Christ who fall into the very common error of assuming that the full blessing of God in Christ must be achieved by their personal effort. They have to do something about it. This mistake of presuming that total commitment, complete consecration is to be achieved by effort on the part of the reconciled soul is widespread. It is almost universal. Paul wrote about this to the Galatians. He called it "salvation by works," and he made it very clear that "by works shall no man be justified" in the sight of God. In fact, in Galatians 3:3 we read,

"Are ye so foolish? having begun in the Spirit, are ye now made perfect by the flesh?"

Now this whole problem of being delivered from the last hold that the natural being has on you, this thing of being delivered entirely from natural ideas, processes, and forces, the whole concept of being set free from the things of this world is brought to the very point when we talk about being delivered from the flesh. This whole problem was demonstrated in the Exodus of Israel. You will remember how the Hebrews were in Egypt and that they were to go to Canaan. The first big aspect of the procedure would be the release of the Hebrews from Egypt.

The final release of the Hebrews from Egypt was featured by two events. You will remember the last plague and the Passover, at which time the guilt of the people was removed. God accepted them. You will also remember that following the Passover was the Red Sea. The crossing of the Red Sea was an event in which the power of sin was removed. Pharaoh represented the forces of human nature, the forces of this world, and he had held all of the Hebrews under his control. When Pharaoh and his hosts were destroyed in the Red Sea, Israel could finally be considered free, and what we saw in connection with those Hebrews coming out of Egypt we can see when we look closer to see those two aspects in the work of Christ.

When we think about the work of Christ, we have in mind the saving of the soul. We remember that He came to seek and to save the lost. He did not come to show man how to do it. He came to save man out of it. This work of Christ was not a matter of His teaching and not a matter of His demonstrating all of the various miracles that He performed. They were important but that is not actually the work of Christ. The work of Christ was featured by two main events: the cross of Calvary and the open, empty tomb. We have to have the dying on Calvary, the resurrection from the dead, and the open tomb. We have to hear the Word spoken as He died on Calvary's cross, "It is finished." And the words spoken by the angels when the women came to the tomb, "He is not here. He is risen."

Those two aspects belong to the beginning of salvation.

One of them reconciles us to God; the other sets us free from this world. You will remember that on the night of the Passover the Hebrews, who were in their homes, had the blood of the slain lamb put on the door post. They were to be dressed, packed, ready to go. You will remember they did go that very night, but their final release from Egypt involved another phase.

Pharaoh had given grudging permission that they might be free to go but he changed his mind. Despite all that he had agreed to, he wanted to keep Israel in bondage. And so we can understand that the Hebrews would never be free until they were out of Egypt, out from under Pharaoh. When we consider what happened to the Hebrews, what happened to the children of Israel in the Exodus at the beginning, we realize that the Red Sea was not an unfortunate barrier that somehow thwarted them. It became the very center of deliverance. That was the experience that set them free. Just as the Hebrews crossed over that portion of the Red Sea on dry land, so Pharaoh, assaying to do the same thing, was destroyed; and in the destruction of Pharaoh, Israel was free from his control. From that time on all the other experiences of the children of Israel had their own part and place as they went along but Pharaoh was no longer involved. Mind you, the influences of Egypt stayed with them for a long time. It has been pointed out that they came out of Egypt in one night but it took forty years to get Egypt out of them.

That is possibly quite true as far as it goes, but I want now to consider what happened at the point of their being set free from the power of Pharaoh. Let us look once more at the empty tomb. When we consider how the body of Jesus Christ was raised from the dead, can you see in that the promise so far as you and I are concerned? Do you realize that what is being shown to us is that as the Lord Jesus Christ went into the grave with His human body dead, God raised Him from the dead never to die again? The forces of this world, the process of living and dying in this world would have no more to do with Him. The cross took away the guilt and reconciled us to God, but the empty

tomb is what releases from the power of evil in the newness of life.

So far as believers are concerned, I realize how very
natural it is for us to emphasize that Christ on the cross
died for me. That is a simple and clear-cut presentation. I
may not believe it, but if I do believe it, I belong. If I
believe that Christ Jesus died for me on Calvary's cross,
there is a profound meaning for me. I am to be crucified
with Christ so that I identify with Him on the cross of
Calvary. At that point I am justified in the sight of God
and accepted in the sight of God, but that is not the whole
story.

One of the great things we should remember is that when
Christ Jesus died on Calvary's cross, He did not die to stay
dead. He died, but He was to be raised from the dead.
Those of us who believe in Him and put our trust in Him
so that we are crucified with Him deny ourselves and yield
ourselves altogether to God. We have the expectation and
the promise that by the power of God we will be raised
from the dead in the newness of life, and we can now live
in this world as the children of God. We can at any time
rest in and trust ourselves to the living Lord Jesus Christ
and have the power of God, the grace of God to help us.

I hope that what I say now will linger with everyone of
us: it is the soul that has died, that can be raised into the
newness of life. First the soul (yours-mine) must die. There
must be denial of self. I must take up my cross. I must die
that I may be raised from the dead. Only the soul that has
died can be raised.

This is very, very important. Many people who hear
the Gospel want to get right with God. They want the
blessing of God, they need the blessing of God, and so they
decide that they will do something about it. What do you
think you will do? What do you think there is to do? I will
tell you what there is to do: yield yourself to God. Turn
yourself over to Him. Just as surely as you do put yourself
in the hands of Almighty God and trust in Him and let
Him have His way with you, you will be finally, fully, and
forever released from the power of this world and the

power of sin. If you fall into sin in the future, and it may happen as long as you have the old man with you, Almighty God will deliver you because you belong to Him.

*Chapter 21*

## COURSE OF SALVATION

Do you realize that the whole course of salvation can be indicated by three prepositions taken in this order: out of, across, into?

God created both earth and heaven. The processes in this world which we commonly speak of as earth follow certain established patterns. They take time and they occur in space; they follow each other in sequence. On the earth things follow each other according to their very nature and throughout all of this law prevails. "Whatsoever a man soweth, that shall he also reap." But there is another world. The other world is heaven. This does not refer to a situation which is true only after I am dead. It does mean that, but "heavenly" also means now; right now heaven is real, just as the earth is real. The processes in that other world, the spiritual, which we also call the heavenly world, are not limited to time and space. This means it does not take a certain amount of time to bring things to pass, nor do those things need any place to happen.

God can do everything He wants to do, any time. Salvation as a work of God is a spiritual operation. He is not limited as we are and in order to show us the plan of His purpose He brought this spiritual procedure down into natural affairs, just as He Himself became incarnate in the person of Jesus of Nazareth. In the incarnation we have this remarkable event taking place: almighty, eternal, infinite God becoming a person in human fòrm, limiting Himself to our size and to our strength, limiting Himself to the body of a man. Something like this is done in Scripture. There the great truth of God which is eternal and infinite, which goes on and on in all directions is revealed through

His servants in His Word when "holy men of God spake as they were moved by the Holy Ghost." So in the written Word of God we have a structure of revelation in language that shows what is actually the mind and the will of God.

We read the Bible for much more than information. In the Scriptures we do get information about certain historic events that took place. There are certain facts recorded with reference to events in this world, and certain facts with reference to people in the world, that make up the history and the biography that we find in the Scriptures, but there is far more than that in the Scriptures. There is revealed in the Scriptures the plan of God as to what He means to do in, by, and through Christ Jesus, and this plan is set before us in such a way that we can see it and understand it.

The plan of salvation, as we commonly call it, is demonstrated for everybody in the Exodus of Israel, and this can be pictured in a diagram. Suppose you took a sheet of paper and on the left at the top put the word "Egypt." Then way over to the right of that sheet of paper, place the word "Canaan." When you look at the word "Egypt" you will remember that is where the Hebrews started and under that you might put the word "bondage" because that was their condition. Now under that word "Canaan" which you have on the right side put the word "freedom." Then draw an arrow from "bondage" to freedom." When you have drawn that arrow from Egypt to Canaan you have made the first sketch of the plan of salvation: out of death into life. That is the way it moves. Salvation brings man out of trouble into rest and peace.

On the left hand side of the page where you had the words "Egypt" and "bondage" it may help to write in the word "slave" and you may add the word "distress." Now with that paper before you, draw two parallel lines perpendicularly alongside the word "Egypt." These will represent a water barrier that was there: the Red Sea. As you thus mark in "the Red Sea" this will remind you that Egypt was bounded by the Red Sea which lay between Egypt and the desert. Later when the Israelites wanted to come out of Egypt the Red Sea was a problem because they needed to cross it to go on their way. When you have done this, look to the right side of your paper and then lower, across the bottom draw two parallel lines and on them put the word "Jordan." This is the river that Israel had to cross finally.

Now you can indicate with little crosses in the region of Egypt the plagues that came upon that country by way of preparing for the release of the Hebrews. For the final plague which was the loss of the firstborn I always put the sign of the cross with a circle around it. That was called the Passover, the big event just before they left the land of Egypt. You can then draw two straight parallel lines from that circle and have them across the Red Sea showing that this is what happened next. When those lines are drawn across the Red Sea I always put some strokes on the other side of the sea, radiating upward. This is to indicate the celebration of deliverance when the Hebrews were led in singing by Miriam.

Now between Egypt which is on the left and Canaan which is on the right you can write the word "desert" or "wilderness." When you look at Egypt you can be reminded that is where they were in slavery; write across that in such a way as to set it apart, perhaps with a red pencil, the words "out of"; that is what the Hebrews were to do with Egypt. They were to come "out of" it. Under the word "desert" you may write the word "across," and so you will have "Out of Egypt" and "Across the Desert." Thus you will come to Canaan. When you come to the land of Canaan, indicate it with an arrow bending down to it and put the word "into" along the arrow. Because Canaan was already there all the Hebrews had to do was to go into it. This will indicate so far as our spiritual life is concerned that the promises of God are already fixed. The plan of God is already settled. All the believer needs to do is to move into what God has already promised.

With this sketch before you, write over by "Egypt" the word "beginning," and then under the word "Canaan" write the word "end." Perhaps you may want to draw a line from "beginning" to "end" in order to show what it means in the book of Hebrews when it says that if you will keep the faith that you had at the "beginning" steadfast unto the "end" you will enter into the promises of God. While you still have that sketch before you, over on the left by the "Red Sea" you can write "conversion" underneath. So far as the "desert" is concerned, underneath that you can write the word "communion," and under the word "Canaan" you can write the word "consecration," because that is what you are coming into in spiritual experience.

The same movement that starts with "conversion" will end in "consecration" if you just keep on believing. And now I will give you three words to place on the very bottom of the page. On the left write the word "come": that is the one word said to the people who were in the land of Egypt. To all people who are in bondage God says "Come." For those who are passing through that temporary period of instruction that is in the "desert," in the wilderness, the word is "Abide," stay with Him. Then on the right by the "River Jordan" with "Canaan" there before you, write the simple word "Go." In those three words, "Come," "Abide," "Go," is indicated the course of salvation.

## Chapter 22

## BITTER WATER

Do you realize that when a person accepts Christ as Savior this does not mean that only good things will happen from then on?

"Accepting Christ Jesus as Savior and Lord" is the way we usually refer to the experience of a person's becoming a believer. Every human being on earth is a creature of God. God made all men, and all men are responsible to Him. All men coming before God are judged according to the deeds done in the body, and they are judged according to the law of God. We are given to understand in Scripture that "no man sinneth not." We are also told "the soul that sinneth it shall die." Because of this it follows, according to the presentation we have in the Bible, that all men are under condemnation. They are altogether found guilty before God.

The Bible points out, in the New Testament especially, that no man in himself can possibly justify himself before God. Nobody is ever going to be able to straighten out his own problem with God. He is already a sinner and already condemned; but "God so loved the world, that He gave His only begotten Son, that whosoever believeth in Him should not perish, but have everlasting life." We call the matter of receiving Christ Jesus as Savior and Lord becoming a "believer in Christ." Accepting Christ Jesus as Savior and Lord is usually a very serious matter. A person may consider such a step for a long time before he takes it. In the world there is trouble, we know, and often there is strain and stress and hurt, and it is this that often prompts many a soul to turn to God for help.

The actual acceptance of Christ Jesus as Savior may be

an occasion of joy to the soul, of gladness to the heart. Quite unconsciously we may naturally assume that now that we have received Christ Jesus as our Savior and Lord everything will be all right. But it does not always turn out that way. This was demonstrated in the case of the Hebrews during the Exodus.

The Hebrews started on their journey. On the night of the Passover they were released so far as Pharaoh was concerned. When they came to the Red Sea the sea was opened up for them to pass through. When Pharaoh tried to do likewise he and his hosts were destroyed. In a remarkable way a cloud hovered over them each day, and as the cloud moved, they moved. They did not know where they were going. The one thing they were responsible for was staying with the cloud, and I have learned to understand how they could do that by remembering that if they just walked in the shade of the cloud they would be following it. The shade would move to the right or the left or ahead or back and they would just stay in the shade and in that way be led across the wilderness. Every night this cloud was a luminous pillar of fire, like something bright and incandescent in the sky, that would lead them.

As they journeyed the first experience that is recorded is that they came to a place called Marah. That word means "bitter water" and that was just the reason it had that name. A spring was there, an oasis, by the roadside where they could drink; but the water was unpleasant to the taste. It was what we would call brackish and this caused real discontent. They did not expect that. They were on their way now and God was with them. They were being led by Moses and he was led by God, and now this water was unpalatable. They complained. They turned to Moses and asked him what they should do. Moses didn't know and he turned to God in prayer, asking for guidance. What happened is very revealing to us: God did not lead them away to a better place where there was sweet water. He did not lead them away from that spot, nor did He change the taste of the water. However, God did do something. He showed Moses that by that spring was a tree; and if he would take a branch of that tree and put it in the water, the water would become palatable.

This is a profound lesson. I wonder if we can understand it right away. What we actually see here is that God is showing them how they can make out where they are. They had been led into a spot where the water to drink was bitter. Now they were to learn that when bitter experiences came and they cried to God for help, the solution was not to withdraw. They were not to turn away and go somewhere else; they should not seek to escape from that spot. There would be an element in that situation that could turn that bitter water into sweet water. This was something they were to learn.

At the next place they stopped there were twelve wells of water, and threescore and ten palm trees a place called Elim, but that came later. At this time there is Marah, this bitter water, and they had to learn how to adjust themselves to a bitter experience. This was the case of the children of Israel. I wonder how quickly we can understand this truth? Can you picture a certain person going to special evangelistic services and hearing the Gospel preached? The evangelist calls on the people who hear to respond, to receive Christ Jesus, and to come forward and indicate their willingness to accept Christ. Can you picture someone doing that and having a great sense of joy because now he is reconciled to God through Christ Jesus and he actually can expect that God will be with him. He may have a great time of fellowship with other believers in that meeting. When he returns home and seeks to share what he has come to believe, he encounters opposition. Some actually turn against him and he now faces bitter experiences.

Think of the man who commits himself to God that he may worship and walk with Him. In his business he wants to be honest in his dealings. He is not going to allow anything to be done that is not fair and square to everybody, including his competitors. He starts living like that, only to find that in no time at all people are objecting to it. There are those who want him to join in some underhanded scheme. Can you realize what happens with a man like that when he no longer will be underhanded? How his own fellow businessmen, his friends, will turn against him? Perhaps there is a youngster in high school who has gone to a special meeting of young people and has accepted Christ Jesus as Lord. He wants to bear witness to his faith, but he runs into ridicule from others. How hard it is for that person!

It is a bitter experience when, for example, you have finally accepted the call to teach Sunday School and find there will be people who criticize the way you do it. Or people will be dishonest or they will be unfaithful to you. So far as you are concerned, all this becomes a bitter experience. Here let us learn: such bitter experiences are in there; they belong to the situation. As a believer you will meet those. The great thing to keep in mind is that the Lord will not lead you away from them; He will not cause you to avoid them. You will be walking with Him when you are led into these things, and you will be with Him while you are in them. Stay close to Him and walk on through them because it is through these things that you really learn how to serve God. And in such situations you really do serve God when you walk with Him in the day of trouble. In every situation you enter as a believer, when you have real trouble there will be an element in that situation that you can use to turn the bitter experience into something sweet by the grace of God.

*Chapter 23*

## HUNGER

Can you understand that hunger is a great blessing?

Blessed are they which do hunger and thirst after righteousness: for they shall be filled (Matt. 5:6).

These words bring a very important truth to our minds. There are many earnest souls who have deep distress because they are so conscious of their unfitness. Sometimes it seems that the finest people we know have the deepest sense of personal unfitness. Perhaps that is part of what makes them so fine, but let me point out that it is an easy thing for an honest person to be discouraged in living because of his own past failure.

There are people who are quite unaware that their record is bad and some people are quite indifferent that their conduct is unfitting. They do not pay any attention to it; they have no interest. They would only be annoyed by talk about being forgiven, about the Gospel. They do not feel that they have ever done anything wrong. I suppose I will have to realize for the time being that I am not counting on those people having much interest in what I am saying. But there are some people who do care. There are some people who actually do suffer because they feel personally unfit. One can think again of Job at a certain point saying to the Lord, "I have heard of thee by the hearing of the ear; but now mine eye seeth thee: wherefore I abhor myself, and repent in dust and ashes" (Job 42:5-6). Or one can think of Isaiah when he had the vision of the glory of God in the temple and he cried out, "Woe is me! for I am undone; because I am a man of unclean lips, and I dwell in the midst of a people of unclean lips: for mine eyes have seen the King, the Lord of hosts" (Isa. 6:5).

102

The apostle Paul could say about himself that he was "the chief of sinners." It would seem that the more sensitive a person is and the more earnestly he cares about being right in the sight of God, the deeper is his feeling of being personally unfit. Therefore Paul could say, "Unto me, who am less than the least of all saints, is this grace given" (Eph. 3:8). Regardless of how depressed such persons may feel in their sense of unworthiness, these folks actually can rejoice because of the promise that is theirs.

I have dealt sometimes with people like that who come to me for help, who are bothered by the fact they just do not think they are worth anything. It is always possible for me to start in with such people by saying that what they feel is absolutely true. And now that they know this we can start there; because if they had not known that we would have had to take time to show it to them. "There is none righteous, no, not one . . . They are all gone out of the way, they are together become unprofitable" (Rom. 3:10-12). That is what the Bible says. When a man feels in himself that he is not fit, he is more than half way on the road to blessing to begin with. No matter how depressing it may be to the heart to be conscious of such shortcomings, such people can rejoice because here is the promise, "Blessed are they which do hunger and thirst after righteousness: for they shall be filled."

We can learn a great deal about this from Israel's experience as the people were starting on their Exodus journey from Egypt to Canaan. When they had come out from the country of Egypt which was their home, they took what bread they had baked with them. In some cases they took the dough that they had prepared for baking the next day, in what they called the kneading troughs, where the dough is kneaded into the shape for the bread to be baked. So these people took their dough and their bread with them as they left home that night of the Passover and started out across the wilderness. But in time they ran short of food.

The food they had when they started was good, but it would not last forever. Some truth will be especially emphasized at the time we accept Christ. We will naturally have that in mind. We accepted Christ with great joy, but more truth will now be needed for daily living. It is the same kind of truth, but it will be different in form. We will need to believe that when Christ Jesus died for us on Calvary's cross we were reconciled to God. But now we need to learn how we can get along with our neighbors, how we can get along with that person who irritates us, or the one who takes advantage of us. We need to know more truth in order to realize that when we put our trust in the Lord Jesus Christ we are depending upon Him. We have to remember that God is in control of all things, including the other man, so that when we yield ourself into the situation, God is over all and will take care of us.

This is truth that we need to learn. The children of Israel had food when they started out on their journey but the time came when they ran short of food. They then came face to face with a very practical problem. There were no resources out there, no place to get anything like meal that they might make bread and bake it. There are no resources for spiritual living in the natural world. This is what the new believer learns. When he starts out with the Lord and has gone with Him for awhile something suddenly happens to present a problem: the way his boss treats him, or the way people in the family treat him, and he has no natural resources of his own to face these things. To turn away isn't good enough. To get angry and to be contentious is not good enough. He needs to patiently trust in the Lord but for that he needs to have particular promises in mind. What happened with the children of Israel was like this: when they were short of food and were faint because of hunger, they turned to Moses and asked him what to do. Moses went to God in prayer and God sent "manna."

Did you know that the meaning of the word "manna" is a question? It actually means "What is it?" In other words, it does not tell what it is, and nowhere in the Bible are we ever told what it is. We know what it looked like; it looked like coriander seed. We know that it appeared on the ground like hoarfrost in the early morning. We know certain things like that. Each day they received a day's supply. Each morning, before the sun was up, they were to go out and collect that day's supply. They were not allowed to stockpile it. They could not go out and industriously collect enough for four days so they would not have to do anything the next three days. If they did collect more than they needed it would actually spoil. So they had to collect the day's supply each morning, except on the sixth day when they were allowed to take two day's supply because of the Sabbath Day, when they would not collect any.

Is there a lesson here for some Bible students who take time out to make a special study of the Bible? They stockpile a great deal of information in their minds and hearts about the Bible and then let it rest there. They do not read the Bible daily. They do not have daily fellowship with God. Such persons may afterward come into a situation where someone will ask a question or some situation will arise when they would like to know the will of God; so they turn to what they know about the Bible but find they do not have anything there which they can use! What they thought was there, isn't there. They thought they had confidence in God but they do not have it. It is as though everything they had was eaten up by termites, so to speak, because they had stockpiled it in a way that was not intended.

The grace of God is something to use. The grace of God is something for me to get this day. I begin the day putting my trust in God and all day long I trust in Him. When night comes I thank God and go to sleep. The next day is a new day. When the new day starts I turn to God again for the day's supply for that day. One is afraid there are some people who have made a thorough study of the Bible at some time, so they have developed a certain understanding of it; then they will teach this over and over again. Have you ever noticed that some of those who know so much about the Bible and can teach it so fluently are often hard to live with? Nobody else can get along with them at all. Do you realize that if people can't live with or get along with others, they are limited? They are actually not showing the grace of God which is in Christ Jesus. Do you know that "When a man's ways please the Lord, he maketh even his enemies to be at peace with him" (Prov. 16:7). Do you realize that when a person is actually living in the way the Lord wants him to live, there will be a quietness and a peace about him that will be attractive to other people and draw them to him?

Whatever you may think, keep this in mind: each day go to the Scriptures. Each day read one more time the original Word of God. Let it speak to your soul and strengthen you as you come to Him in prayer and faith, that you may have His blessing.

*Chapter 24*

## THIRST

Do you realize some personal fellowship with the living Lord is essential for a strong, triumphant faith?

> As the hart panteth after the water brooks, so panteth my soul after thee, O God. My soul thirsteth for God, for the living God: when shall I come and appear before God? My tears have been my meat day and night, while they continually say unto me, Where is thy God? When I remember these things, I pour out my soul in me: for I had gone with the multitude, I went with them to the house of God, with the voice of joy and praise, with a multitude that kept holyday. Why art thou cast down, O my soul? and why art thou disquieted in me? hope thou in God: for I shall yet praise him for the help of his countenance. O my God, my soul is cast down within me: therefore will I remember thee from the land of Jordan, and of the Hermonites, from the hill Mizar. Deep calleth unto deep at the noise of thy waterspouts: all thy waves and thy billows are gone over me. Yet the Lord will command his lovingkindness in the daytime, and in the night his song shall be with me, and my prayer unto the God of my life. I will say unto God my rock, Why hast thou forgotten me? why go I mourning because of the oppression of the enemy? As with a sword in my bones, mine enemies reproach me; while they say daily unto me, Where is thy God? Why art thou cast down, O my soul? and why art thou disquieted within me? hope thou in God: for I shall yet praise him, who is the health of my countenance, and my God (Ps. 42:1-11).

These are the words of the psalmist: a great outcry, a great expression of an inward longing. He wanted to have fellowship with God. He wanted to know God. Believing persons are prone to fall into an unhappy error. So often the matter of accepting Christ has been developed and expressed as a matter of understanding. Then people will try to explain and to show how these things are. The whole matter becomes a matter of logical argument and rational explanation, as if that was what mattered. The believer who should be witnessing to what the Lord has done, to what He is doing, and how wonderful it is to have fellowship with Him starts to explain what the Gospel means in rational terms. Instead of calling souls to "come to the Savior, make no delay, here in our midst, He is standing today, tenderly saying 'Come'," he begins to direct the listener as to what he should do. Such a waste of time and such a misdirection of interest and effort! The problem is not a matter of understanding. It is not a matter of engagement in some task. The problem of the individual soul is a matter of personal acceptance of Christ as Savior and communion with Him as the Lord.

Let me put it this way. A husband may know quite well who is his wife, and he may know what he needs to do to support his home, but knowing all that will not build a home. The husband needs to have association with his wife. He needs to be in communion with his wife. That is the foundation of the home. The great poet Edgar Guest has a line that I often think of, "It takes a heap of living to make a house a home." That is just the point. Personal communion with the Lord is like water to a plant, to a bird, or to any creature on earth. Good plants may be growing in rich soil, but they can wither and die right there on the ground if they are without water. It takes water to make that good soil available to that plant. Thus it is with believing experience. The secret of much distress and the secret of much weakness on the part of people who really want to follow the Lord is their lack of communion with Him. They do not take time to be with the Lord. They try to work out something on their own. They get involved with other people. They discuss and plan with other people and work along with other people. They are disappointed and hurt by other people. But wait a minute. All those other people do not matter. Where is the Lord? What is your relationship with Him?

By the way of contrast let me point out a practical procedure that will promise blessing. Take your Bible and locate certain passages to read which you can feel bring you into fellowship with the Lord. Mark those passages. Read them again and again! Working with the Lord and for Him is good, but that kind of working will wear you out. You will get to where you are weary of the whole business. You need to look into His face. That will strengthen you and enable you to belong to Him.

After the children of Israel had the experience of being hungry and being provided for by the manna from heaven, they came to a place where they had no water. Being without water and having thirst is the sharpest and most acute distress of all. A person can go a long time being hungry but not nearly so long being thirsty. I suppose that what we need most of all is air, then water, then food — in that order. We are just now thinking about thirst: thirst is not only a great desire and a longing; the thirst is actually providential because feeling thirsty will cause you to seek water. You need it. Without water you will wilt like a plant in the garden.

Why then shouldn't you and I understand that for ourselves? We may have the understanding of the Scriptures so that we have a full, clear understanding of what the Bible teaches, but if we do not have personal fellowship with the Lord our soul will wilt. I need water to drink. He said, "I am the Water of Life." He said again about those who come to Him that "out of their inward parts shall flow rivers of water." This you can have if you will have personal fellowship with the Lord. Paul wrote in II Corinthians 3:18, "But we all, with open face beholding as in a glass the glory of the Lord, are changed into the same image from glory to glory, even as by the Spirit of the Lord." What Paul is saying is that as we look into the face of the Lord Jesus Christ we shall be changed into His own likeness by the Holy Spirit of God.

How important this is! I am concerned about those who feel weak. They feel worn out, depleted. Do you know what that reminds me of? Some plants are growing in spots where they get no water but the leaves look wilted.

They will fold when the plant becomes limp. and unless water is provided they will die. And so it is with reference to the Lord Jesus Christ. Look into His face. It has been said that one look is enough to save the soul but it is gazing on His face that will sanctify the soul; and that is what we have in mind right now. The thirst that we can feel in our soul is for the living God — to have fellowship with Him.

*Chapter 25*

## CONFLICT

Are you prepared to accept the idea that living by faith as a believer in Christ in the will of God will involve the believer in conflict?

> For we wrestle not against flesh and blood, but against principalities, against powers, against the rulers of the darkness of this world, against spiritual wickedness in high places (Eph. 6:12).

This is not exceptional. This is not something only some believers do. Paul is implying that all believers "wrestle not against flesh and blood." Our real problem is not other human beings who do not agree with us or who do not understand us, but against principalities, against powers, against the rulers of the darkness of this world, against spiritual wickedness in high places.

It is a sobering reality that if a person accepts the Lord, believes in the Lord Jesus Christ as Savior and Lord, and begins to live in obedience to the will of God, he will have to face opposition. Sometimes the opposition will be personal, sometimes human, but always it will be spiritual and that means undying opposition. There is no way in which a believer can avoid this.

The Lord Jesus Christ faced this opposition right down to His death on Calvary's cross, and "the servant is not greater than his master." Just as surely as Satan opposed Jesus Christ to the very last, he is going to oppose you and me if we dare to believe in and walk in obedience to the will of God. Often the opposition does not develop in terms of face-to-face confrontation. We cannot always get the enemy to stand right up and oppose us. This is what I often think about with reference to Bible teaching and Bible interpretation. It is not the out-and-out contradiction to the Bible that we need to fear. We can deal with that. It is the insinuation, the half-and-half suggestion. It is the intimation that something else could be true even though no one tells you what it is. This weakens the disposition to stand fast and challenges every one of us. If the enemy would openly accuse the Lord or would openly deny the Lord, if the people who criticize the Bible would only point out something wrong in it, or if they would just come right out and say, "This is a mistake or that is a contradiction," but this is not their style. They will hint. They will suggest. They will lift the eyebrow or shrug their shoulder in a way that implies, "There is a lot here that is not like it is supposed to be."

What are these things that are untrue? The critics will not face that. They are inspired by a subtle and cunning enemy who pursues the believers to cut off the weak ones. Such opposition is inspired by Satan, who is an incorrigible foe of the Lord Jesus Christ. "He goeth about as a roaring lion seeking whom he may devour" among believers. All of this was vividly demonstrated in the experience of the people of Israel in their Exodus from Egypt on their way across the desert, when they were pursued by an enemy called Amalek. Amalek would follow at a distance and cut off the stragglers. Moses dispatched Joshua to engage Amalek in battle and to bring him out into an open straightforward fight. He succeeded in this but when Joshua led the forces of Israel against the Amalekites something happened that was very sobering. Amalek could win. So far as this world is concerned, if you are thinking of a knockdown, drag-out fight between that which is good and that which is evil, and if you think, in a pious fashion, that those that are good are going to win, you are mistaken. In this world evil has all of the advantages. The evil is pulling the believer in a downhill drag while the believer is trying to pull uphill. It is a hard thing in this world to walk straight with all the forces against you pulling the other way. We are in enemy territory. As a matter of fact, the opposition to living the life of obedience to God is just so great no human being in himself can succeed.

In this battle between Joshua and Amalek, Amalek could prevail over Joshua; but that isn't the whole story, fortunately. Moses went to the top of a hill to pray, to raise up his hands in prayer. Then was revealed a wonderful truth. As long as Moses prayed, Joshua could win. You might say, "Now that is fine; victory is as good as in the bag." But not so fast! Moses was just a human being and he grew tired. When Moses' hands were heavy so that they came down, Amalek started winning. This is not at all encouraging. But that is not the whole story. Aaron and Hur came to help Moses. Aaron was Moses' brother and Hur was one of the leaders of the Israelites. He is mentioned in one other passage of Scripture but there is nothing notable about him. Neither Aaron nor Hur were what would be called extraordinary men. Neither could fight like Joshua nor pray like Moses. But they rolled up a stone for Moses to sit on because he was tired, and they held up his arms while he prayed until the going down of the sun. When they held up his arms, which means they joined him in intercessory prayer. As long as they did that, Joshua prevailed, and the result was that on that day Joshua won a notable victory. It is a matter of note in the eternal record that the forces of God can win the victory over the forces of the enemy.

This was a great experience for Israel. They learned something. In a battle of the forces of righteousness against the forces of evil the secret of victory is united, intercessory prayer. Joshua had to fight and Moses had to pray, but Aaron and Hur had to join in prayer to bring victory. I often ask myself, "Who won that battle?" We must remember Joshua was fighting for his life, and they could not have won without him; but he would have been defeated. Moses' praying was very important: "The effectual fervent prayer of a righteous man availeth much" (James 5:16); but he would have quit. He grew tired and I want to tell you right now it is a hard thing for a tired man to be good. The outcome depended on Aaron and Hur. They could not fight like Joshua and they could not pray like Moses, but they held up the hands of Moses, and thus the victory was won.

Do you realize that everyone in your family who believes in the Lord Jesus Christ is facing an enemy who is subtle, powerful, and scheming? Do you realize that the only way we can claim the victory for them is through prayer? And are you aware of the fact that good people can get tired of praying? What shall we do? We should join, get together. We should have prayer partners. You and someone else should pray together. If that someone else could be in your own family, it would be wonderful. But if not, join with someone else. Unite your hearts in intercessory prayer. "Again I say unto you, That if two of you shall agree on earth as touching any thing that they shall ask, it shall be done for them of My Father which is in heaven" (Matt. 18:19). In this whole matter of conflict with the forces of evil, the secret of victory is not personal strength. It is not personal virtue. It is praying to the living God. United intercessory praying is the key, the secret of victory.

## Chapter 26

## HUMAN LIMITATION

Do you realize a person can hinder his own work by undertaking to do too much?

We have kept in mind all the way through our study that salvation is the work of God. This is something that God does. You will remember that the word "salvation" means everything that is done in the human being by the work of the Lord Jesus Christ. We have noted that the plan of salvation is revealed in the Bible, and we understand it is for us to know about and to believe. If it were not important it would not be there. The Bible deals with eternity and time, with heaven and earth. It is not a big book when we consider that it is dealing with so many various items, but what is in there is important. One of the things set forth in the Bible clearly and plainly is the whole work of salvation of God's saving souls through the Lord Jesus Christ. The plan of salvation is pictured for us in the experience of Israel and we understand that the Exodus of Israel out of Egypt across the desert into Canaan is the authorized demonstration of salvation for our learning.

Just now we are noting events that happened to the children of Israel as they journeyed, and thus far we have noted four events. We have been studying recently how after they started out they came across bitter water. Shortly after that problem was solved they had no bread; and it was the manna from heaven that saved them. Then they had no water and the rock was broken open and water gushed forth. They then came into a deadly conflict with Amalek which was won through united, intercessory prayer. After that another problem arose in a rather strange way. Moses' father-in-law, Jethro, who was from the country of Midian, came to visit Moses and his family, but was unable to see Moses because he was busy from dawn to dusk dealing with the people coming before him.

> And it came to pass on the morrow, that Moses sat to judge the people: and the people stood by Moses from the morning unto the evening. And when Moses' father-in-law saw all that he did to the people, he said, What is this thing that thou doest to the people? why sittest thou thyself alone, and all the people stand by thee from morning unto even? And Moses said unto his father-in-law, Because the people come unto me to inquire of God: when they have a matter, they come unto me; and I judge between one and another, and I do make them know the statutes of God, and his laws. And Moses' father-in-law said unto him, The thing that thou doest is not good. Thou wilt surely wear away, both thou, and this people that is with thee: for this thing is too heavy for thee; thou art not able to perform it thyself alone. Hearken now unto my voice, I will give thee counsel, and God shall be with thee: Be thou for the people to God-ward, that thou mayest bring the causes unto God: and thou shalt teach them ordinances and laws, and shalt shew them the way wherein they must walk, and the work that they must do. Moreover thou shalt provide out of all the people able men, such as fear God, men of truth, hating covetousness; and place such over them, to be rulers of thousands, and rulers of hundreds, rulers of fifties, and rulers of tens: and let them judge the people at all seasons: and it shall be, that every great matter they shall bring unto thee, but every small matter they shall judge: so shall it be easier for thyself, and they shall bear the burden with thee. If thou shalt do this thing, and God command thee so, then thou shalt be able to endure, and all this people shall also go to their place in peace. So Moses hearkened to the voice of his father-in-law, and did all that he had said. And Moses chose able men out of all Israel, and made them heads over the people, rulers of thousands, rulers of hundreds, rulers of fifties, and rulers of tens. And they judged the people at all seasons: the hard causes they brought unto Moses, but every small matter they judged themselves. And Moses let his father-in-law depart: and he went his way into his own land (Exod. 18:13-27).

It is important to read this entire account so that we can feel the situation it describes. Let us now note what is revealed here. Sometimes sincere people among us suspect that organization is something unspiritual. They are inclined to say that if we are serving the Lord and being led by His Holy Spirit we will not have to make any plans about it. Everything will work out. To be sure, some organization may be unspiritual. There may be occasions when people get together to work as human beings and organize themselves to get something done when the people interested and the purpose of the whole project may be unspiritual. That is possible, but sharing responsibility in service can be of God. You and I should keep this in mind especially if we reach the point where we are going to do something in the Lord's work. If we have any responsibility in working for the Lord that is what we should remember.

Let me show you how it is described in the New Testament. Someone may say, "That is Old Testament material. That is the way they did back in those days before they had the Holy Spirit, but believers would not need to do that now."

> And in those days, when the number of the disciples was multiplied, there arose a murmuring of the Grecians against the Hebrews, because their widows were neglected in the daily ministration. Then the twelve called the multitude of the disciples unto them, and said, It is not reason that we should leave the word of God, and serve tables. Wherefore, brethren, look ye out among you seven men of honest report, full of the Holy Ghost and wisdom, whom we may appoint over this business. But we will give ourselves continually to prayer, and to the ministry of the word. And the saying pleased the whole multitude: and they chose Stephen, a man full of faith and of the Holy Ghost, and Philip, and Prochorus, and Nicanor, and Timon, and Parmenas, and Nicolas a proselyte of Antioch: whom they set before the apostles: and when they had prayed, they laid their hands on them. And the word of God increased; and the number of the disciples multiplied in Jerusalem greatly; and a great company of the priests were obedient to the faith (Acts 6:1-7).

The believers wanted to win people. They wanted to bear testimony to the Lord. Because many believers were together, they had become confused and the confusion, of course, caused misunderstanding; criticism and contention followed. That was not good so Peter, speaking for the apostles, directed organization. He wanted them to select seven men from among themselves, and the apostles would appoint them to this work of supervision. They would attend to practical matters and allow the apostles to be free to go on with their praying and their preaching. "We will give ourselves continually to prayer, and to the ministry of the word." That is the way it happened there in New Testament times.

This brings us to a very simple conclusion. The work of the Lord is not one man's task. It is for all. All believers share in it. To be sure, one person may be spokesman but the others are with him and they join him. If any one person is alone that is not good. It is not good for him and it is not good for other people. This matter of organization is a rather significant thing because if a person is going to share his responsibility and service, he has to humble himself. He has to allow that someone else can do this, too, and someone else should help him. This has been variously expressed and I think probably could be expressed as well as anything if I were to say this: someone has pointed out that is is better to put ten men to work than for one man to do the work of ten.

This is very important for all of us. Just let us keep one thing in mind: it is possible to undertake so much we don't do it well. It would be far, far better trusting in the providence of God and following His guidance, that we do that which we can do and leave others, actually assign to others, that which they can do, because the work of the Lord is for all of us. May the Lord help us in our wisdom about these matters.

## Chapter 27

## MT. SINAI

Can you understand that a person must receive some guidance in order to be able to obey the Lord?

We are continuing in our study of the whole truth of salvation, particularly as it is pictured in the experience of the children of Israel when they were brought out of the land of Egypt into the land of Canaan. As we follow them on their course we are learning what salvation means for us because, of course, salvation is the work of God that brings the human heart and soul to Himself for blessing, and this will be shown forth in actions and in conduct. Coming to God is not a matter of geography, coming to a certain part of the country; it is not even a matter of position, to the right or to the left, up here or down there. Coming to God takes place in a person's heart when he yields in his heart to the reality of God and is inclined to walk His way. To be blessed of God is to do His will; God will bless those who obey Him.

Just now I want to point out to you that to want to do the right thing is of course very important, but in itself this can prove disappointing because one might want to do the right thing and still not get anything done. Why? Because he would not know what to do. Then we see that to know what to do is most important and most significant. Any man thinking about God and seeking His blessing realizes that he must obey God to be blessed. God has a will. He is a living God. He wants us to walk with Him, and if we let Him be in us He will move in us to will and to do His good pleasure.

Here something important comes to light. What God wants me to do is not always what I think I ought to do, or what I think I can do, or what I think I will do. What

God wants me to do is not even what I conclude would be a good thing. I have no way of knowing what God wants me to do; He must show me the way to go, the thing to do. He must show me what to say, how to think. You will remember when God called Samuel as a child and Eli gave him this advice: "Go, lie down: and it shall be, if he call thee, that thou shalt say, Speak, Lord; for thy servant heareth" (I Sam. 3:9). This is what we need to do.

We are going to look now at the children of Israel as they were in the land of Egypt, coming out to go to the land of Canaan. Let us keep in mind what the situation is. These Israelites had been in bondage. Remember, they were slaves. Can you realize that as slaves they were not free to do as they pleased? They were slaves to pagans so it stands to reason their conduct and their way of doing things would be largely controlled by pagan people. This means these Hebrews would have no experience in godliness. They would have no way of knowing what would be pleasing in the sight of God. Isaiah refers to this: "For my thoughts are not your thoughts, neither are your ways my ways, saith the Lord" (Isa. 55:8). There was something the Israelites needed to understand. Because God was holy they would have to be holy. This word was spoken to them very clearly, "Be ye holy, for I am holy, saith the Lord."

How were they going to do that? What does this mean? The word "holy" has something to do with their conduct, with their manner, their style of living. They were to live in such a way as would be agreeable to God. What would that mean? God is a certain kind of person: the same yesterday, today, and forever; and God in Himself is holy. He would not accept anything that isn't holy. We can conclude that out of the experience of having been delivered from the land of Egypt, being set free from their bondage, there would be in their hearts a natural disposition to want to do the will of God, to be well pleasing in His sight. Since they were out there in the desert where they were so dependent upon everything around them, they would want the continued blessing of God. Here we have people who really want to have the blessing of God and for that they want to know what God wants them to do. In the course of their travels they came to a place called Mt. Sinai, where they camped for many months. Here they were instructed. Moses went to the top of the mount and, praying, had fellowship with God. While the children of Israel were encamped about the mountain, Moses went to the top of the mount and for forty days he was unseen, not heard from, out of sight. He was communing with Almighty God and receiving from God the revelation of how these children of Israel were to be instructed so far as their conduct was concerned.

When you instruct you come with a pattern that you want to have established. You "structure" it, very much the way in which a woman would take a bolt of cloth and with a pattern structure the cloth into a dress or shirt. The Israelites were minded to do the will of God but did not have any idea what to do, so Moses instructed them. He showed them the structure of the kind of righteousness that would be acceptable to God. This was shown to him on the mount. We will be thinking about that and consider how he received the law of God. After he had received the law of God, which was the pattern of what would be acceptable to God, he could come down and show them "This is the way God wants you to do it." But because these people were, after all, human beings you know what was going to happen. They would not keep the law. Even if they wanted to, they couldn't. So they would break it. They would sin.

Moses received from God another pattern, another revelation. God showed him the conditions under which a sinner could come into His presence. This was shown to the children of Israel in the form of a building called a tabernacle. It was a building that had in it certain articles of furniture and a route marked for the worshiper to come to God. The worshiper would come through the tabernacle with the several articles of furniture, which would indicate to the sinner what he should do that he might come out of himself in his sin into the presence of God in His holiness. This is pictured in the tabernacle.

But who would lead the sinner to do what he should? The slaves would not know what to do. These people without any background would not know what to do. God called certain men out to be priests, and Moses and Aaron taught these priests what to do in order that they could lead the children of Israel in their worship to God. They learned from the beginning that no man could come by himself. The sinner needed to bring a sacrifice. There was an outline of the various sacrifices they should bring, and there was a description of the way in which to do it, that you and I would call a ritual.

All of this was revealed to Moses during the forty days on the mount. This revelation was not given to him in order that the children of Israel might be reconciled to God or that they might come to God, but because they were reconciled to God. They belonged to Him; but they did not know how they could live to be pleasing in His sight. This was revealed to them on Mt. Sinai. There they were instructed in that which would be acceptable in the sight of God.

*Chapter 28*

## TEN WORDS

Can you see the importance of guidelines in living and doing?

> And thine ears shall hear a word behind thee, saying, This is the way, walk ye in it, when ye turn to the right hand, and when ye turn to the left (Isa. 30:21).

These words are a promise from Almighty God to His people, who put their trust in Him and wanted to walk with Him. Salvation takes place in the human being by the grace of God. God is working in them. What does He do? Does He change their appearance? Does He make a man bigger or smaller than he was before? What, then, does God do? He guides them in the way to be pleasing in His sight. The one thing that matters is the way in which a person goes, what a person does. All the ways of man are open and above board before God, who looks into the heart.

One of the problems in living for all of us is very simple. When you wake up in the morning you haven't been through that day before. Things will come up you did not expect. There will be things you did not know about because you have not been over this road before. Many persons are frustrated even when wanting to do the right thing. They do not know what to do. They do not know which way to go. They want to do the will of God. How can they know what to do? Sometimes, not knowing what to do, a person will look to others to see how they are going. But in all of this there is uncertainty because the ways of God are past finding out and, as we have previously noted, His ways are not our ways. His thoughts are not our thoughts. Many times well-meaning people, good people, are frustrated in themselves and filled with uncertainty and doubt. They do not know for sure which way to go, because not every possible way of doing things is good. Not every alternative will lead them where they want to go and not everything they might do will lead them where they ought to go. The dynamic to move a person, giving him the inward disposition to want to go, is essential. I need in my heart, to want to do the will of God, but I need also to know where to go and what to do.

The children of Israel were slaves in the land of Egypt, and they were having trouble. They were being persecuted so that the matter of coming out of Egypt was not very complicated. All they wanted was to get out of there. It did not make so much difference to them at the time which way: just any way, out of there. That is often the feeling when troubles are involved. Actually entering into Canaan was more of a problem because the question then would arise: what would be the right thing, how should one do this? What should be done that would be acceptable before God? They needed to know these things.

When the children of Israel came in their travels to Mt. Sinai they stopped for some time. Moses entered into prayer with God. He went to the top of the mountain and was unseen and unheard of for forty days. After that time he came down with two tablets of stone saying that the finger of God had written Ten Words on those two tablets of stone. That phrase the "Ten Words" is the biblical phrase for what is commonly called the Ten Commandments. Actually the idea of the "Ten Words" is more precisely the biblical idea. There were many more than ten commandments in the Old Testament. The Jewish culture recognizes 613 commandments in the Old Testament. I believe they find as many as 13 commandments in those Ten Words.

Consider the Ten Words that are commonly called the Ten Commandments — what do they signify? They are a simple, clear description of what God requires of man, that man might be acceptable in the sight of God. The two tablets were flat pieces of stone, the tops of which were curved like an arch, in oval fashion. They were generally always seen together, with four letters on the first one, in

# THE TEN WORDS

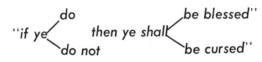

"if ye ⟨do / do not⟩ then ye shall ⟨be blessed" / be cursed"⟩

## The Law of God

Roman numerals, and six on the second one. Thus the first four commandments were on one tablet and the last six commandments on the other, which is very interesting because later when Jesus of Nazareth was asked what was the greatest commandment He said, "Thou shalt love the Lord thy God with all thy heart, and with all thy soul, and with all thy mind" (Matt. 22:37). The first four words, commonly spoken of as the first four commandments, all deal with God. The last six have to do with man, so when the Lord was asked what is the first and great commandment He said, "Thou shalt love the Lord thy God and the second is like unto it, thy neighbor as thyself."

These words, these commandments, do not have in them the power to motivate action; they have in them the power to guide action. They do not make man do anything but if he wants to do something they will guide him into the right way of doing things. They are like a fence. You can't get anywhere traveling on the fence but the fence will keep you out of the ditch. It can be a good guide.

When I have had driving to do in the mountains, especially at night, it has been wonderful to have guidelines on the pavement or to see a fence with whitewashed posts on the side of the road which actually guide us by showing where the road is. These Ten Commandments were not given to bring man to God. They were given to willing men to guide them how to be blessed. If a person wants to know how to be blessed, he should look to the Ten Commandments. The first four commandments will show how to reverence God and the other six will show how to honor those who are in authority, to be considerate of your equals and charitable to the poor. Here is the outline of what would be counted right in the sight of God. If a person were minded to do it, that is the way.

The meaning of all this was expressed in a formula. It is very simple. If a person does what God requires, he will be blessed. If he does not do what God requires, then he will be cursed. Both results come from God. God does make beans grow in the garden but He also makes weeds grow on the lawn. He does make wheat grow in the field, but He also makes thistles grow in the fields. When the wheat grows we call it blessing, and when the thistles grow we call it cursing. The words "blessed" and "cursed" are very much alike. They indicate God increasing the matter, whatever it is. If you do what is right, it will be increased, you will be blessed. If you do what is wrong that negative part will be increased and you will be cursed. You will suffer loss.

Chapter 29

TABERNACLE

Do you realize that doing the right thing involves doing it the right way?

> But without faith it is impossible to please him: for he that cometh to God must believe that he is, and that he is a rewarder of them that diligently seek him (Heb. 11:6).

It sounds so simple when anyone wants to know what the Gospel has to say about coming to God, to say "Only believe." Now the question is "Believe what?" or "Believe whom?" Believing is like swallowing. No man can live by swallowing alone. I am sure that every man who starves to death is swallowing, but if he does not have something to swallow he will die. It is swallowing food that keeps the body alive and that keeps it strong. So it is in this matter of salvation, of believing the Gospel that one might be saved. One must believe the truth about Jesus Christ. That is what one must believe, but what is that truth about Jesus Christ? How would one know it? It is not just His name. His name could mean anything that a man might think about it. But that is not the point. That would not be the truth.

The truth about Jesus Christ is revealed in the Bible. When we talk about being saved by faith, we mean saved by believing what the Bible teaches about Jesus Christ. It is possible to see how the truth about Jesus Christ is revealed in the pattern of the tabernacle. We have already taken note that while at Mt. Sinai Moses received the law of God in the Ten Words, two tablets of stone on which were etched by the finger of God the Ten Words that we commonly speak of as the Ten Commandments. This would be important when the sinner would want to come to God. The law of God contained in the Ten Words would reveal sin, and the soul that sinneth it shall die, but it was possible by

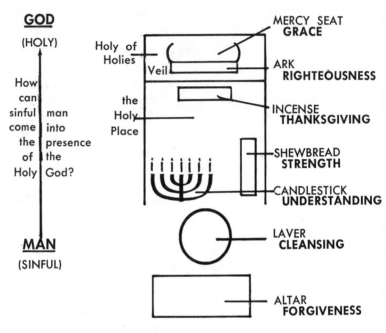

## The Tabernacle

the grace of God for a sinner to come to God. This is what we are now going to see.

The tabernacle was a sort of building designed to be used as a place of worship. At first it was made of skins and was a tent, but later the same pattern was made into a temple, made of stone and wood. It was arranged to show how a sinful man might come into the presence of a holy God. The tabernacle was a building that was somewhat rectangular and had two parts. The open part into which the priest first entered was called the "holy place." A little beyond the middle there was a veil, a curtain that shut off an inner compartment. Past that veil was the "Holy of Holies," or "the Holiest of All."

In the Holy of Holies was the Ark in the center, and in the Ark was the law or the Tables of Stone. On top of this Ark were two creatures made of gold that looked like birds; they were called cherubim. They represented angelic creatures. Between the two there was an open space that was called "the Mercy Seat." That was where God would meet with the worshiper face to face, as a man speaks to his friend.

In the courtyard out from this building was the altar, the place where they brought the sacrifices. When a man came to worship God he would bring a lamb. He would bring this innocent creature to that altar. The priest would have the worshiper place his hand on the lamb's head and confess his sins on the lamb. It was understood then that the guilt of this worshiper was transferred to the lamb. The lamb was a substitution for the worshiper. The law said "the soul that sinneth it shall die" so that because of the sin of the worshiper death should take place. But God would allow a substitute to be used — this innocent lamb. The priest would then take the lamb and kill it. The blood would be sprinkled inside the tabernacle, inside the holy place, and afterwards inside the Holy of Holies itself. Confession took place at the altar and was followed by forgiveness.

No doubt there are many sinners who come to worship God today and this is as far they ever get. They confess their sins and they are forgiven; that is wonderfully true but that is not all they should do. Between the altar and the tabernacle itself was a round structure, which looked like a washtub on stilts. It was called a "laver" and it was filled with water. This would show that when the worshiper had come to the altar, confessed his sins on the lamb, and the lamb had been slain so that the worshiper was forgiven, the worshiper should then come to the laver where he would be washed and cleansed.

In the matter of cleansing we should note some important things. Only the confessed, forgiven sin can be cleansed. A man cannot be cleansed of sin he has not confessed.

After that the worshiper came to the holy place, which was an area with an open entrance. On the left was a seven-branched candlestick, bringing to mind "light," and that brings to mind understanding. When we add this up we find that the worshiper comes to the altar, confesses his sin, comes to the laver, is washed and cleansed from his sin, and now he receives understanding of the grace of God. On the right side opposite the candlestick was the smaller table called the table of "showbread." On that were two pots of manna reminding the children of Israel how they were fed with manna every day for the forty years in the wilderness. That represents food, and food brings strength. Thus there is light and food at the same time. It is always significant that when we have more light, we have more strength, and when we have more strength, we have more light, more understanding.

Further up and close to the veil there was a smaller altar. This was incense or perfume. This indicated the praise of the worshiper, the thanks of the believer. Coming into the presence of God the sinner would come to the altar, confessing his sins and being forgiven, then he would come to the laver where he was washed and cleansed, then past the candlestick, where the light would shine into his heart and understanding, and past the showbread, where he was reminded where he could get food and strength. Finally he came to the altar of incense and gave thanks to God.

Since the death of Christ the veil has been taken away and believers can now come into the very presence of God to the mercy seat. There at the mercy seat the worshiper meets God face to face, and God will deal with him in grace and mercy even though he was a sinner. But his sin is now forgiven and cleansed, and he now understands about the grace of God and gives praise and glory to God, so that God deals with him as a man deals with his friend. That is the way the children of Israel were taught to worship God. It is still a good way for us.

*Chapter 30*

# PRIESTHOOD

Can you see why it would be important for a person who came to worship God in the tabernacle to have a guide?

It is a wonderful thing to realize that God not only provides what we need for salvation but He sends a guide to lead us directly into His blessing. This could be seen in the case of the children of Israel. In the matter of worshiping God we noted in our last study how He revealed to Moses the pattern of the tabernacle where they were to worship God. In it were certain articles of furniture, each one of which represented some aspect of what was involved when a soul would come to God.

Now we shall notice that He not only had that building planned but He guided Moses in the matter of arranging to have guides to lead the people through the building to God because the sinner would not know what the various things meant. It may seem to some people that it would have been sufficient that the sinner would want to come, and that was important, but coming to God would be acceptable only under certain conditions. Let us just say very kindly that not anybody can come to God any way he may want to. There is a right way to come to God. God provides free salvation but always under certain conditions. The layman turning to God on his knees and in his guilt would not know what those conditions are. Even those of us who have read and heard about them need to be helped, and certainly the man who has never read or heard about them would not know how to do.

Moses showed the pattern of the tabernacle that had been revealed to him on the mount, a building in which the sinner could come to worship God by doing certain things.

It could be understood that the layman would not know what those things were, so the plan was that there should be certain chosen persons who would guide the worshiper and represent him in the process. We have a word for that in our culture — "advocate." If you have ever been in court you know there are many aspects of the law that the average person would not know, so he has a lawyer to stand up for him. He is called an "advocate." That idea is taken over in the New Testament to refer to Jesus Christ. John said, "My little children, these things write I unto you, that ye sin not. And if any man sin, we have an advocate with the Father, Jesus Christ the righteous" (I John 2:1). We have Someone in the presence of God who will appear for us and who will bring our case before God.

There are several things about the priests in the Old Testament that are of importance to us, and as we are studying salvation we should keep them in mind. Believers have been made by the Holy Spirit into being kings and priests before God. So every believer in the Lord Jesus Christ has the function of a priest to perform with reference to other people. It would be a wonderful thing if every Christian would help others to come to God. The Old Testament priests were of the family of Levi, being the sons of Aaron. Several things were said about them in the New Testament. No man took this privilege in his own will. He was called, commissioned of God. In the Old Testament he was born in that family and that is how he received this responsibility. In our day and time we have been born again and we have that responsibility given to us, not because we chose it, not because we thought we wanted it, but because God wanted us to have it. This was said about them in the New Testament. In Hebrews 5:1-2 we read, "For every high priest taken from among men is ordained for men in things pertaining to God, that he may offer both gifts and sacrifices for sins: who can have compassion on the ignorant, and on them that are out of the way; for that he himself also is compassed with infirmity." That was the kind of person who was chosen.

All this was pictured in the Old Testament, especially in Exodus 29. The procedure was described by which these priests were set aside to be consecrated to their office. Several things that were done could be meaningful to us. Moses was to take these sons of Aaron and wash them with water. The man who was to serve as a representative of the truth, and who was to explain the truth to others and lead them, should himself be washed with water, which meant that he had repented of his sins and that he was a person who humbly and with a contrite heart had committed himself to do the will of God. They were to be anointed with oil. This can point to the coming of the Holy Spirit. He was to be washed so far as his sins were concerned and was to be anointed with oil so far as the Holy Spirit was concerned. We would say today if anybody was going to do the will of God he should forsake his sins, be washed with water, and personally accept and receive the Holy Spirit of God.

There were then three things to be done with him. A sin offering was to be presented. This man was just a human being and would himself sin though he was going to serve God. If he would sin, what then? Would he be disqualified? No. That is one of the wonderful things about the Gospel. No sinner needs to feel himself disqualified if he is willing to confess his sins and to bring in the sacrifice of Jesus Christ on his own behalf. Just as the sin offering was received by the priest so, when I come into the presence of God even now, what would make me fit would be that so far as I know and so far as my heart and mind are concerned, I have forsaken those things in me that I believe would be displeasing to the Lord. I have sought to receive from God the consciousness of His presence and the anointing with oil, and I am daily counting on Christ Jesus' interceding on my behalf. He is my sin offering always in the presence of God, always offering Himself for my sins in order that they may be taken away.

Next, there was to be a burnt offering, which seems to imply the dedication of the whole personality to God. It was like consecration. In the sin offering sins were forgiven but the burnt offering meant yielding of oneself in toto to God. Then a very graphic part of the ceremony took place. They were to be blood marked. One of the animals brought by the priests was killed, blood was taken, and the priests were marked. Interestingly enough, the blood was placed on the tip of the right ear, on the thumb of the right hand, and on the toe of the right foot. What does this mean to us so far as personality is concerned? What do you do with your ear? You listen. The tip of the right ear would mean that that person would listen to the Word of God, to the guidance of God. Such a person is to be subject to the guidance of Almighty God in His Word. What do you do with your hand? There are two things you do with your hand: primarily you work; you may also say you greet people. You shake hands with them. Back in the Old Testament days a person worked with his hands. What is the significance of having blood on the thumb of the right hand? What a person does is done as unto the Lord. You are blood marked in your action, in what you actually do. Then blood was put on the toe of the right foot. What do you do with your foot? You walk. This means that the foot itself would be marked with blood. So here is a priest who is going to listen with his ear blood marked. He is going to work with his hand blood marked and he is going to walk in the presence of God with his foot blood marked. The priest is to be a person who is totally given over to God because Christ Jesus died for him. Before the ceremony was over an offering was put into the hand of the priest and he was told to offer it up to God. (Even when the priest serves he does not do so by his own efforts or wisdom. He is given from God what he needs to serve God.) All of this is significant to us when we remember for ourselves that believers are now priests unto the Lord.

LISTEN
WORK
WALK

*Chapter 31*

## THE OFFERING

Can you understand how a person who has offended another may want to bring some gift by way of compensation so that good relations might again be established?

> For every high priest taken from among men is ordained for men in things pertaining to God, that he may offer both gifts and sacrifices for sins (Heb. 5:1).

We say salvation is the work of God. That is true. It becomes even more meaningful when we remember that God is a person. Sin is doing wrong like bumping into a stone wall is doing wrong, but in that case you just hurt yourself. In sin there is an offense against a person. You offend God. It is more than displeasing. The Bible tells us God is angry with the wicked every day. The Gospel reveals that Christ Jesus came into the world to reconcile the sinner to God. That means the sinner was so far out and God was so far away that Christ Jesus came to bring them together and to reconcile the sinner to God.

It sometimes seems to me that well-meaning persons picture God's grace as being such that everybody can come to God any time and in any way. That kind of teaching and preaching is in error. We should represent God as He is. We are glad to tell people God is merciful; we are glad to tell them He is gracious and kind. We need to be very careful that we do not leave the impression that God is soft. The only things we know about God are set forth in the Bible. The Bible does tell us plainly that a broken and a contrite heart God will not despise, and we praise His name for that; but God resisteth the proud and so we humble ourselves before Him.

Some try to picture the Old Testament as being faulty

because it shows the wrath of God whereas the New Testament shows the love of God, as if that were something else; but this is not a true impression. Often people interpreting the Bible feel free to cast aspersions; some actually question Paul or Peter, James or John when these men of God emphasize in their writings that God is not mocked, that "whatsoever a man soweth that shall he also reap." But the wrath of God is just as real as the grace of God; and Paul wrote about both in Romans. The book of Romans is a wonderful book to show how a sinner can be saved by simply believing in the Lord Jesus Christ, that righteousness is a gift from God which God gives to anybody who believes in the Lord Jesus Christ; yet in the first chapter we find three different conditions under which God lets His wrath abide upon the unbelieving.

The Scriptures reveal that Jesus Christ, the Righteous, is the propitiation for our sins, and not for ours only but also for the sins of the whole world. What do we mean when we say that? It means that the Lord Jesus Christ did something that so affects God that God is kindly disposed toward us, not because we deserve it and not because our sin is the less terrible, but because Christ Jesus did something that affected God that way. If you feel that makes God something very much like a human being you will have to remember that language is very limited and we human beings are limited in our effort to understand God.

The point is that when man sinned he offended God, and God's attitude toward him is going to be an attitude of judgment. The sinning man has something coming in judgment. But Christ Jesus came to propitiate God, to affect God by His conduct in such a way that God will look kindly and mercifully upon this wrongdoer.

The whole idea of bringing a sacrifice to God is central in the Bible and in the Gospel of the Lord Jesus Christ. For instance, at the beginning of the whole Bible story we have the case of Cain and Abel, who came to worship God. They brought sacrifices to God as we would bring a present to a person with the idea of influencing that person to be kindly disposed toward us. When Noah came out of the ark after the flood, he built an altar to worship God and sacrificed

clean animals before God. This practice was followed all
through the Old Testament. You will remember so far as
Israel was concerned that their whole experience in Egypt
climaxed on the occasion of the Passover. But the central
item in that event was that a lamb was put to death, and
the blood was sprinkled on the doorposts. We say that
Christ Jesus is our Passover Lamb.

In the instructions that Moses received on Mount Sinai,
when he was telling the people of Israel how they should
live when they went into the land, he outlined to them that
the priest should bring offerings to the Lord in worship.
Each offering in the Old Testament presents some aspect
of the work of Christ Jesus. What Jesus Christ did for me on
Calvary's cross includes everything that the offerings of the
Old Testament spelled out for people.

There are various parables of the Gospel in the New
Testament; for instance, the story of the sower and the seed,
which tells how the seed fell on different kinds of ground
and the different results. We read the story of the net that
was thrown into the sea which brought in all kinds of fish.
There is the story of the man who sowed wheat in the fields
and the enemy came and sowed tares. Each parable shows
some aspect of the Kingdom of God. They are all true. We
can learn from each of those parables, because together
they all show the salvation work of the Lord Jesus Christ.
It is like this with the sacrifices.

In the book of Leviticus we read in the first chapter about
the burnt offering. What is implied in this? The burnt offering was one in which the whole animal was burned — meat,
skin, bones, everything, and this says to our hearts that
when Christ Jesus came to offer Himself for us He came
totally. There was no reservation. He committed Himself
altogether. The burnt offering is an illustration of consecration with nothing withheld, with everything given over
to God. In the next chapter we read about the meat or meal
offering, an offering of food. The significant thing about
that was that it should be made of fine flour. Have you ever
handled flour in your fingers and recognized when it is fine?
You press the flour between your fingers, move them back
and forth, and if there is no grit you say it is fine flour. This

signifies the perfect life Christ Jesus lived, in complete obedience. After the meat offering, the peace offering was made by fire. The animal was brought in and burned. In that we can see how the Lord Jesus Christ endured suffering for us.

There is one of the offerings which to me shows something very wonderful. The priests were told to bring an offering for the ignorant sins of the people, because the people committed sins they did not even know about. Because of sin they would be unacceptable to God. So the priest would offer a sacrifice for the ignorant sins of the people, the sins they did not even know they committed. I love to think that is what the Lord Jesus Christ did for me. He came to offer Himself for me and He died for me to take away the guilt and the responsibility even of those things I did not know were wrong. By the way this is where we can feel that children are included in the atoning work of Christ because there was actually an offering made for the ignorant sins of the people, and this applies to the conduct of infants.

Finally, in that list there was a trespass offering, an offering made for people who knew they had done wrong. They were to come in and confess the wrong they had done, confessing their sins upon the sacrifice that they brought in. Thus the sacrifice would suffer for their sins.

This quick review of certain things that are implied by the various sacrifices in the book of Leviticus illustrates that each one represents some aspect of the death of the Lord Jesus Christ. The wonderful thing about all of that is when the worshiper brings the offering to the priest and the priest makes atonement for him for his sin, the sin shall be forgiven. Christ Jesus came to reconcile us to God by suffering for our sins and carrying them away. Almighty God is a real being. He is a personal being. He is a holy being. He is offended by my sinful conduct, but when Christ Jesus comes and dies for me in such a way that when Almighty God looks upon His Son, He is propitiated, He is inclined to be merciful and kind to me for Christ's sake.

*Chapter 32*

## RITUAL OF WORSHIP

Do you think it really makes a difference if a man stands up and takes his hat off when the national anthem is played?

"Draw not nigh hither: put off thy shoes from off thy feet, for the place whereon thou standest is holy ground." These words are found in Exodus 3:5 and they are recorded as the Word of God that was spoken to Moses. We are noticing at this time what happened to the Israelites when God called them out of Egypt into the land of Canaan. We feel that things happened to them for examples and are written for our learning. We see now how God is bringing His will to pass and calling Moses unto Himself. At this point we find Almighty God impressing something on Moses' heart and mind.

Let us notice again these words as they are written in Exodus 3:5. One could wonder at this point what a man should do if he were going to turn to God. Can any man at any time just turn to God in any way? Now listen as God speaks to Moses, "Draw not nigh hither: put off thy shoes from off thy feet, for the place whereon thou standeth is holy ground." We are all acquainted with the custom of all present in a courtroom standing while the judge enters and takes his seat. We know what it is like in school when children have their daily exercises, including, among other things, the salute to the flag and the repetition of the oath of allegiance. Then all face the flag and the hand is placed over the heart. We know, too, that it is a mark of gentility when men arise if a lady enters the room. We train our children to say "please" and "thank you," "excuse me" and

139

"I beg your pardon." Such conduct we believe is wholesome. It is good for everybody.

Not only are these things a matter of being polite but they are a matter of being courteous and respectful. When such response or such action is directed toward God we call it reverence. This can be expressed in certain procedures. It is not enough to say simply, "We should reverence God." The question is "How?" Because what one thinks about God greatly affects how one trusts Him. So we ask ourselves how we shall think about God — what we shall think about Him. We have some common practices that I suspect pass without notice, yet they point toward God. Two of them are actually prescribed by God Himself and are taken from Scripture. We know that one day in seven is called the Lord's Day, a matter of apportioning time. We are acquainted with the fact that the Bible seems to teach that one tenth of one's money is what God would require; we are thus using our means to serve Him in the tithe. We can be assured that if anybody or any family will habitually, regularly, earnestly, and honestly practice the observance of the Sabbath and paying the tithe, such persons will be blessed.

By common consent we have other practices. It is a common thing for us if we are coming into the presence of God to go to our knees. We bow our heads before God. These are attitudes of humility. Again, by common consent when we are praying it is the custom for us to shut our eyes; in so doing we shut out the world and we are alone with God. Our church buildings are for the worship of God, and the sanctuary, meaning the holy place, should be accorded our respect. I am very much inclined to think that a church building is not a place for games of any kind or any activity other than the worship of God. It is set aside for that purpose.

We think of the public worship services we have which again are our custom. At a specified time of day we come to church and are given a program called the Order of Worship. As we come in we will probably see in the front of the church somewhere near the pulpit an open Bible. That indicates something. From the Word of God we get our message.

Usually the communion table is in the front of the building and here we gather for the sacrament. In the general practice of the church there are at least two sacraments. We have baptism and we have the Lord's Supper. There are different views of baptism and I think there are different views of the Lord's Supper. We should remember that Christ arranged for this: "This is my body broken for you. Take, eat, do this in remembrance of me," and again, "This cup is the New Testament in my blood, shed for many for the remission of sins. Drink ye all of it." These are instructions given by the Lord Jesus Christ, the doing of which was set out before us to emphasize His significance.

In Old Testament times when the children of Israel were coming out of Egypt they were to learn how to have fellowship with God because God was going to dwell among them in the land of Canaan. There was in the tabernacle a certain outline shown in the very furniture, but Moses gave them a ritual to follow. That procedure was followed through according to those articles of furniture. The worship of God started at the altar outside the building in the courtyard. There was an altar where the worshiper would come with his sacrifice; there he would confess his sins on the sacrifice, after which this sacrifice, perhaps a lamb, would be killed and the blood sprinkled in the tabernacle on behalf of this man. This is a way of picturing that a human being could come into the presence of God on the basis of the death of an innocent substitute. This applies in the present time when we as believers come into the presence of God not because we are worthy but because we trust in the Lord Jesus Christ, confessing our sins.

That was the first step. The next article of furniture the worshiper met was the laver, that washtub on stilts between the altar and the tabernacle filled with water, at which place the worshiper was washed. This indicated cleansing and meant that he was to forsake sinful practices. He would be forgiven sinful practices at the altar because he confessed his sin to God on the head of the animal but now, at the laver, he would be washed clean. On his left was the candlestick. This would indicate to him he should have light and we know "the entrance of Thy Word giveth light" so we have no difficulty realizing that this is a way of saying the confessed sinner who has forsaken his sin should read the Bible. On the right hand was the showbread which would strengthen him. He should meditate on the Scriptures because the Lord Jesus is the bread of heaven, and meditate on the Scriptures, "chewing them," as it were, to get the message to his own being. In front was the altar of incense where there is praise and thanksgiving. From there he could go into the very presence of God, face to face, at the mercy seat.

Here, then, is outlined a procedure beginning with the confession of sins, going on with the forsaking of sins, reading the Scriptures, thinking about them, thanking God for His blessing, and beholding His face: a ritual to follow whereby the worshiper could come into the very presence of God.

## Chapter 33

## JUDGMENTS OF MOSES

Do you think a believer is free to do anything he wants to do if it is not expressly forbidden in the Bible?

> Then one of them, which was a lawyer, asked him a question, tempting him, and saying, Master, which is the great commandment in the law? Jesus said unto him, Thou shalt love the Lord thy God with all thy heart, and with all thy soul, and with all thy mind. This is the first and great commandment. And the second is like unto it, Thou shalt love thy neighbor as thyself. On these two commandments hang all the law and the prophets (Matt. 22:35-40).

Keeping the commandments of God is something far more than obeying the letter of the law.

There is no doubt that some people have thought there was liberty for certain activities that they want to follow because they discovered those activities are not expressly forbidden in the Bible. Let me ask you this question, "Do you think it would be wrong for a believer to speed in his auto through a residential area by saying to you that autos are not mentioned in the Bible?" Or would it be wrong for a believer to use drugs and say to you, "Well, drugs are not mentioned in the Bible," or would it be wrong, for instance, for a person to go to a public place of amusement and bet on the outcome of a horse race or a football game and say to you that is not mentioned in the Bible? Horse races, football games and other things are not mentioned in the Bible and you can understand right away how unsound such an approach would be.

The Ten Words that Moses received on Mount Sinai did not specify any acts as such. Those Ten Words may be summarized, as was done by Jesus of Nazareth when He pointed out that the first great commandment was "Thou shalt love the Lord thy God" and the second "Thou shalt love thy neighbor as thyself." I sometimes sketch the whole meaning of the Ten Commandments in four requirements. I point out that in the first place these Ten Commandments require of man that he be reverent to God; in the second place, that he have respect for those in authority, in the third place, that he show consideration for his equals, and in the fourth place, that he exercise charity on behalf of the poor. Those four ideas, reverence, respect, consideration, and charity, will in a general sense cover all that we have in the Ten Commandments. Today people do not find something right or wrong because that particular activity was described in the Bible. They can see that something is wrong if it is not reverent, if it does not respect those in authority. Conduct is wrong if it is not considerate of our fellow man, and conduct is wrong if we do not exercise charity toward the poor. Whatever the situation, we can apply these principles of judgment.

Even in the time of Moses application was necessary. In the Pentateuch — the five books of Moses — we find, especially in Exodus and then afterwards in Leviticus, Numbers, and Deuteronomy, there will be many judgments of Moses, many instances and situations in which he gave a judgment as to what should be the conduct one should follow in some practical situations, such a thing, for instance, as finding our neighbor's ox in the ditch. The Ten Commandments do not specifically talk about oxen, so what shall we do if we find our neighbor's ox in the ditch? Moses would tell us to get that ox out of the ditch. Suppose we find the neighbor's ox straying on the countryside. Do we have a responsibility? Moses would say yes, we do have responsibility. The Ten Commandments do not say so but application of their principles lead us to conclude these things.

Exercising his judgment in such matters took up Moses' time. In each case he had to think through those problems. Situations would arise such as how to treat another man with whom you have quarreled or how to treat your wife. Moses became so preoccupied he did not have the time to visit with anybody. Afterwards he divided his responsibility among others. Today, living on this side of Pentecost when the Holy Spirit has been given, we are much more fortunate than Moses was. We do not have to feel our way along to see how the various principles of the Ten Commandments would apply. We have the Holy Spirit in our hearts who will make us conscious of the judgment of the living Lord Jesus Christ. The Holy Spirit will guide us and show us and will comfort us as we go along with Him. This is what He is to do. Jesus of Nazareth rose from the dead and ascended into heaven. He gave His Holy Spirit to be in our hearts and by His Holy Spirit the mind of the living Lord Jesus Christ is communicated to us. We are prompted from within as by the Spirit of God in the very will of the living Lord in the things that we are to do.

We find that Paul, for example, said, "Wherefore, my beloved, as ye have always obeyed, not as in my presence only, but now much more in my absence, work out your own salvation with fear and trembling. For it is God which worketh in you both to will and to do of his good pleasure" (Phil. 2:12-13). It is very important to notice that when Paul says "work out your own salvation" he does not say "work for your own salvation." We are not supposed to do these things in order to be saved but since we are saved we are to yield to Him and work it out. We work out our salvation very much in the same way a woman with a piece of linen that is stamped for embroidery stitches patiently so that the pattern, when it is worked out, is the same pattern that was stamped on the linen to start with.

You and I have stamped upon our hearts and minds the very thoughts of Almighty God in Christ Jesus. This all begins very simply. We are yielded to God and we want above everything else to be pleasing in His sight. The Lord Jesus Christ said, "My Father worketh hitherto, and I work . . . The Son can do nothing of himself, but what he seeth the Father do: for what things soever he doeth, these also doeth the Son likewise" (John 5:17-19). And if I have His Spirit in me I have no other interest than simply to do whatever I am inwardly prompted to do as by the living Lord Jesus Christ through His Holy Spirit. Paul had this in mind when he wrote "And whatsoever ye do in word or deed, do all in the name of the Lord Jesus, giving thanks to God and the Father by him" (Col. 3:17). Now doing things in the name of the Lord Jesus will mean that we are actually yielded to Him, living with Him, working with Him, and letting Him work out His will in us.

So whatsoever you do in word or deed, you do all as led by the living Lord Jesus Christ, giving thanks to God and the Father by Him. You do not go by rules; you go by the Lord. Paul indicates his own frame of mind in II Corinthians 5:9: "Wherefore we labor, that, whether present or absent, we may be accepted of him." Now that rather stilted English language can be translated properly and well if we say it like this, "We are ambitious to be well pleasing in His sight." And this is what marked the life of the apostle Paul. He yielded himself to this and in himself admitted this one thing — he was ambitious to be well pleasing in the sight of his Lord. This is the way those of us in whom salvation is being worked out by the power of God will find that we are led. We are not led by rules or regulations, we are led by the fellowship we have with the Lord and by His Holy Spirit, who prompts us to feel "This is the way, walk ye in it."

## Chapter 34

## ORDER IN THE CAMP

Do you realize that to be blessed in freedom requires that a person should be under control?

In the apostle Paul's writing to the Corinthians we read,

> For though I be free from all men, yet have I made myself servant unto all, that I might gain the more. And unto the Jews I became as a Jew, that I might gain the Jews; to them that are under the law, as under the law, that I might gain them that are under the law; to them that are without law, as without law, (being not without law to God, but under the law to Christ,) that I might gain them that are without law. To the weak became I as weak, that I might gain the weak: I am made all things to all men, that I might by all means save some . . . I therefore so run, not as uncertainly; so fight I, not as one that beateth the air: but I keep under my body and bring it into subjection: lest that by any means, when I have preached to others, I myself should be a castaway (I Cor. 9:19-22; 26-27).

It is the most natural thing in the world for a person to want to be free — free to do anything, free to do whatever one wants to do at any time. Some have tried to make a way of life out of this. They would indicate that they think the right way to do things is to do what comes naturally. In fact, at one time a great French educator tried to practice this. He had a theory that the best way for people to learn was to do everything naturally and it was said that he allowed the shrubbery in his yard to grow as it would without pruning. With the trees not trimmed, we can picture about how everything turned out. Anybody who has raised tomato plants knows the extra shoots must be pinched off, and if you want good apples you must prune the trees.

When in school you must choose your bibliography and read books that are in the courses you are taking. If you keep a house in a decent fashion you are going to have a place for everything. Anybody who has ever accomplished anything knows that you must select the things that are helpful and avoid the things that waste time and energy.

Now all of this is true in living. God made this world. He made it just as it is and He made us able to work. When Adam was put in the Garden of Eden, he was told to dress and keep it. It was his business to look after it. We need to realize this is the same principle that is true in spiritual living. We need to realize that doing things in an orderly fashion — this thing here, that thing there, this thing now, that thing later — is spiritual. This is of God. It would be easy to think that if God is in a program we will not need to make arrangements. We can just go ahead and expect God to take care of the outcome. That is not true! Let's put it this way: God taking care of it means that He has put you in it and you can think. God taking care of it means that He put you in charge and you can arrange priorities.

This was illustrated in the case of the children of Israel when they were being brought out of the land of Egypt, across the desert, to Mount Sinai. At Mount Sinai God had revealed to them through Moses instructions about living, the Ten Words that we commonly call the Ten Commandments. And He had revealed to Moses instructions about worshiping Him, how a sinner could come into His presence as in the tabernacle, and how to do things right in the ritual of worship. Now He is going to show them something else. He tells them how they are to arrange themselves. Whenever they made camp they were to place the tabernacle in the center and to the north would be three tribes, to the east would be three tribes, to the south would be three tribes, and to the west would be three tribes. This was done each time they camped. When they traveled, three tribes were to lead off, then the Levites were to bring the outer parts of the tabernacle, three tribes were to go next, then the Levites were to bring the ark, followed by three tribes. In the rear guard there were three tribes. This was done each time; always the same way. They were learning each has his place and each was to take his place and that was what made progress possible.

In salvation, when I am walking with the Lord, I will be led into arrangements that are actually structured. This is to be done here, that is to be done there, this is to be done now, and when this is shown to me and I am to walk in that way, you can see how this sort of arrangement demands humility on my part. That may not be what I want to do. I may not want to do what I am told to do, and I may not want to go where I am told to go. How many people have a feeling that if they were allowed to do things themselves they would do well! They think they would do so gladly and willingly, but that is not true. Actually, if I am not given some kind of order in which to do things I would not get anything done.

By the way, what have you ever seen done by people that was a good thing to look at? Have you enjoyed seeing a parade? Which would you rather see — a big crowd of of people in some motley fashion stumbling along irregularly or a parade of men who have been trained? The same would be true, for instance, if there were a group of people with various musical instruments. Do you think it would be pleasing if they all made noise at the same time or do you think it would be better if each played his instrument in an organized fashion so that there would be a rhythm that produced stirring music? This could be done only if they had a bandmaster. The same is true in all areas of life. A group of people each doing what he wanted to do, singing what he pleased, saying what he pleased, could produce bedlam. But that group could be organized with a director and the result would be music that is pleasing to the ear.

All this could be repeated over and over again. Everything worthwhile has been accomplished with structured arrangements. This is true spiritually. I want to emphasize at this point in our study of salvation that if I am being saved I will do what I am told, where and when I am told; and I will be blessed.

*Chapter 35*

## CLEAN AND UNCLEAN

Since God made all things, would not everything be all right?

"And that ye may put difference between holy and unholy, and between unclean and clean" (Lev. 10:10). This is the way Moses instructed the children of Israel. They were told that they were to do this because they were going into the land to live with God, and He was going to live with them. There was one word given to them very clearly, "Be ye holy for I am holy, saith the Lord." To this end Moses gave them certain instructions.

There is a loose idea abroad that since God made everything, all is the same with Him. The truth is that we label things. We name things because we do not consider all things are alike. God will deal with things as we name them. Some things are helpful and we say they are good. Some things are hurtful and we say they are bad. It is a mark of intelligence to put distinctions between things where there is a difference. A word in our vocabulary these days is very much suspect. People don't want to use it. It is the word "discrimination." But do you know what discrimination really means? It is based upon insight in which we see that some things are good and some things are bad. And it is a mark of intelligence that in our thinking and handling of things we put distinctions where there really are differences. Not all things are alike. This is illustrated when we think of the many bottles on the shelves of a drugstore. When the druggist receives a prescription from a doctor he takes from these bottles certain ones that are designated. Some have in them ingredients that are poison

150

and actually some parts of those are in the prescriptions they made up. But everything is according to plan.

Now let us consider what Moses needed to bring to the children of Israel. They had lived as slaves in a country that was pagan, where they were not in charge. Things were done to and for them according to what their masters would indicate. Now they were on their own, so to speak, and they were going to live in the presence of God. They needed to learn how to do it. They needed a frame of mind in which they would be able to reject evil, and that frame of mind needed to be cultivated. Moses injected a concept of the unacceptable, the unclean, into their consciousness. The words he used were "clean" and "unclean." This was sometimes a matter of sanitation and sometimes a matter of hygiene, but often it was a matter of regulation: that which was done the way it ought to be done was clean, and that which was not done in the way it ought to be done was unclean. He brought this idea of clean and unclean into all aspects of their life, even so far as their food was concerned. To this day among their descendants we know that they speak of certain foods being "kosher," and that word means clean, all right to eat.

In checking these things from a scientific point of view, from an actual chemical analysis and a dietary point of view, it has been brought out that the rules that were described in the Pentateuch with reference to food are very wise rules. Not only was this true about habits of food but in personal habits. There were ways to conduct themselves which were clean and other ways would be described as unclean, and they were given the strictest instructions about this. The same was true with reference to their schedule. Moses brought out the fact that one of the seven days was to be a Sabbath Day and on that day there were certain things they were not to do. This was a definite instruction rigidly enforced because he wanted to bring into the minds of these people the idea that some things will do and some things will not do. If they did on the Sabbath Day things they were not supposed to do they were punished.

The same is true with reference to family life. They were given instructions about marriage, about conduct between husband and wife. It was all spelled out in an open, plain way. To do one way would be good and acceptable, to do differently would not be acceptable. The words he used were clean and unclean — even in the matter of divorce. Divorce was not God's first choice and would not have been the thing He wanted for them, still because of the hardness of their hearts Moses allowed them to divorce each other, but only under certain conditions, by following certain laws. There was a way to do it that was right and a way that was wrong. The whole idea is some things are right, some things are wrong. Do what is right and you can expect blessing; do what is wrong and you can expect cursing.

In the control of servants the same is true. Although the servant would be a slave, there were things the master had to do for this servant that were right and if he did not, the master was punished. This applied also to neighbors. They were definitely told how to conduct themselves. In all of these lesser matters in living that I am mentioning one idea was brought to the forefront all the way through: was the activity clean or unclean? Would God approve or disapprove? These guidelines were almost like instructions for children.

To this day many times people will say, "You are not supposed to place restrictions on anyone. You should never inhibit or prohibit anyone. A person should be free." When I was studying an advanced course in psychology at the university, our professor was belaboring this point, that any kind of prohibition did not have any educative value, that one could not learn by prohibiting, by inhibiting. One could only learn by doing things. By way of stirring the class up toward the end of the course, he turned to me because he knew all along I had not been able to follow him since I did not think he was right. He asked me point blank, "Don't you think that any kind of prohibition or restriction would actually interfere with learning?" When I was asked that question in a graduate course in psychology from a professor from whom I wanted to get a grade, it called for an answer, for a discussion. I answered: "That sounds very good and I am quite sure that on the surface it would seem to be true. But that is like telling me that in handing a boy a gun it would not be important to tell him it was loaded. We could let him find out. Actually, I will admit he can find out. But it could be very expensive." This would be the same as if a person were to go into a drug store and take all the labels off the bottles, so that the customer could be free to take anything he wanted to have. That would be a good way to get into trouble.

So far as life is concerned, we need to be very careful to select the right things and avoid the wrong things. The question, "Is it clean or unclean?" is basically important, and it can be stated even better by asking, "Would God approve or would He disapprove?" The truth is that if God would approve it, you will be blessed. If God would disapprove it, you will be cursed. All of this is related to the fact that "no man liveth to himself alone."

## Chapter 36

## GOLDEN CALF

Do you think it is possible for a person who has become a believer ever to be deceived and led into ungodly action?

In our study of salvation we want to learn all we can about the work of God in our hearts. We learn by studying the Scriptures to see how He dealt with Israel "for these things happened to them for examples: and they are written for our admonition, upon whom the ends of the world are come" (I Cor. 10:11). We will focus our attention upon an incredible event in the history of Israel. After being delivered from Egypt by the power of God these people were led in the desert daily by cloud and at night by fire. They were fed by manna. They drank water from the rock and they were given victory over their enemies in battle. Would you think that such people could turn from God? As a matter of record they did, and it all happened naturally.

The people made camp around Mt. Sinai. Moses went to the top of the mountain, where he was in communion with God for forty days. During that time the people began to lose confidence in Moses. There was a feeling that they did not know for sure what had happened to him, or where he was. We read that the people said to Aaron, "Make us gods, which shall go before us; for as for this Moses, the man that brought us up out of the land of Egypt, we wot not what is become of him" (Exod. 32:1). They needed something to put their trust in so they asked Aaron to make gods for them. Aaron told them,

> Break off the golden earrings, which are in the ears of your wives, of your sons, and of your daughters, and bring them unto me. And all the people brake off the golden earrings which were in their ears, and brought them unto Aaron. And he received them at

their hand, and fashioned it with a graving tool, after
he had made it a molten calf (Exod. 32:2-4).

The significance of the golden calf is related to the culture of Egypt. As previously mentioned, the Hebrews had
lived in Egypt for four hundred years. The Egyptians were
animal worshipers. They worshiped oxen and calves, so,
when Aaron made them a god in the form of a calf, we can
understand the cultural influence. He made a god like the
gods of Egypt: a golden calf; then he told the people,
"These be thy gods, O Israel." The Hebrews "rose up early
on the morrow, and offered burnt offerings, and brought
peace offerings; and the people sat down to eat and drink,
and rose up to play" (Exod. 32:6). What a description of
human beings doing what human beings want to do!

When Moses was in communion with Him, the Lord
said upon the mount, "Go, get thee down; for thy people,
which thou broughtest out of the land of Egypt, have cor-
rupted themselves: they have turned aside quickly out of
the way which I commanded them: they have made them
a molten calf, and have worshiped it, and have sacrificed
thereunto, and said, These be thy gods, O Israel, which
have brought thee up out of the land of Egypt" (Exod.
32:7-8). Then He said to Moses, "Let me alone, that my
wrath may wax hot against them, and that I may consume
them: and I will make of thee a great nation" (Exod. 32:10).
But Moses besought the Lord in prayer: "Turn from thy
fierce wrath." Moses told God that if He did destroy the
children of Israel, the people of the world would not understand it; they might think that God started something He
could not finish. He prayed further, "Remember Abraham,
Isaac, and Israel (Jacob)." These are the men whose names
represent faith in God. Abraham had believed in God;
Isaac had believed in God; and Jacob had believed in God:
and the promise made to these forefathers had been that
God would save their people, Israel.

When Moses argued this way in prayer the Lord repented
of the evil that He intended to do and indicated that He
would spare the people. When Moses came down and saw
the people carousing around the camp, eating and drinking,

he threw the Tablets of Stone on the rocks and smashed them. This was a display of righteous indignation. It might seem at this point that Moses became angry, that he lost his temper. Moses did not lose his temper; he showed his temper. He showed them that their conduct had been offensive to God. What they had done was to break the very law he was bringing down to them, and so in a dramatic way, in a very fitting way, he smashed the law right before them.

Moses called Aaron and questioned him about what had been done. Aaron answered, "You know how it is with the people. They insisted on doing something like this and they brought all of their jewelry and gold together and I put it into this big kettle and there came out this calf." Aaron made it sound as if he was not responsible. But Moses judged him for it. Moses ground up that calf and dissolved it. Then he made the people drink the solution. After that he called to the people, "Who is on the Lord's side?" The Levites lined up beside him; whereupon he armed them with swords and set them on the other people. The result was that 3,000 people were killed. That sounds terrible. It *was* terrible. It may seem that was a terrible thing for Moses to do, but it was terrible for the children of Israel to turn away from God as they did.

When they disobeyed and dishonored God, the only way in which they could be cleared of that sin was to be judged. In that judgment 3,000 people were killed. But then the record tells of the marvelous thing that happened when Moses returned to the Lord. "And it came to pass on the morrow, that Moses said unto the people, Ye have sinned a great sin: and now I will go up unto the Lord; peradventure I shall make an atonement for your sin" (Exod. 32: 30). He was going to pray for them. Moses returned unto the Lord and said, ". . . Oh, this people have sinned a great sin, and have made them gods of gold. Yet now, if thou wilt forgive their sin —; and if not, blot me, I pray thee, out of thy book which thou has written" (Exod. 32:31-32).

In this way Moses showed that he really cared for these people, and they really belonged to him. He had judged them as they deserved, but now he wanted them to be forgiven. The Lord said unto Moses, "Whosoever hath sinned against me, him will I blot out of my book. Therefore now go, lead the people unto the place of which I have spoken unto thee: behold, mine Angel shall go before thee: nevertheless in the day when I visit I will visit their sin upon them" (Exod. 32:33-34).

This whole story reveals the marvelous truth about that faithful man, Moses. The people had disobeyed him, had ignored him, and turned away from him. He faithfully confronted them with what they had done, judged them for their wrong, and then went to Almighty God and prayed for them. This is guidance for all believers. It will work with any friends; it will work with your family. When you come into the presence of God on behalf of your people you do not give up; you continue to hold them before God, asking Him for mercy and for kindness toward them, though you may confess their sin to be real.

*Chapter 37*

## BUILDING OF THE TABERNACLE

Do you think if a person wants to serve the Lord there is any need for him to be well trained?

There seems to be a popular idea that if a man serves the Lord in honesty and sincerity he need not know much; the Lord would teach him what he needs to know. I will raise this question again. If God is leading me to serve Him, will He not show me how He wants me to do things? As a matter of fact, He does show me. For instance if He wants me to build a house and He is going to lead me in this, He will show me how to learn to be a carpenter, a bricklayer, and a painter. If He leads me to drive my car to a distant city, and I am trusting in His providence, He will show me where to get a map so that I will know where I am going.

All of this was seen in the building of the tabernacle in the wilderness. You will remember these people had been slaves and not many of them were skilled laborers, yet some learned while they were slaves how to do things. So we read how God led Moses in the matter of having these people get together and build the tabernacle. We can learn a great deal from this. When Moses had called the people to begin building the tabernacle, the record is:

> And they came, every one whose heart stirred him up, and every one whom his spirit made willing, and they brought the Lord's offering to the work of the tabernacle of the congregation, and for all his service, and for the holy garments. And they came, both men and women, as many as were willing-hearted, and brought bracelets, and earrings, and rings, and tablets, all jewels of gold: and every man that offered offered an offering of gold unto the Lord (Exod. 35:21-22).

> And all the women whose heart stirred them up in
> wisdom spun goats' hair (Exod. 35:26).

> The children of Israel brought a willing offering unto
> the Lord, every man and woman, whose heart made
> them willing to bring for all manner of work, which
> the Lord had commanded to be made by the hand
> of Moses (Exod. 35:29).

Believers are moved from within to be willing. Believers
do not have to be persuaded; they only have to be given the
opportunity. The Holy Spirit working in their hearts will
prompt them to want to serve the Lord.

> And Moses said unto the children of Israel, See, the
> Lord hath called by name Bezaleel the son of Uri,
> the son of Hur, of the tribe of Judah; and he hath
> filled him with the spirit of God, in wisdom, in un-
> derstanding, and in knowledge, and in all manner of
> workmanship (Exod. 35:30-31).

God had prepared this man. Moses recognized this man,
called him forward and placed him in charge.

> And he hath put in his heart that he may teach, both
> he, and Aholiab, the son of Ahisamach, of the tribe
> of Dan. Them hath he filled with wisdom of heart, to
> work all manner of work, of the engraver, and of
> the cunning workman, and of the embroiderer, in
> blue, and in purple, in scarlet, and in fine linen, and
> of the weaver, even of them that do any work, and
> of those that devise cunning work (Exod. 35:34-35).

God had prepared these men and at the proper time He
brought them forward and gave them the inward wisdom
they needed.

> Then wrought Bezaleel and Aholiab, and every wise-
> hearted man, in whom the Lord put wisdom and
> understanding to know how to work all manner of
> work for the service of the sanctuary according to all
> that the Lord had commanded. And Moses called
> Bezaleel and Aholiab, and every wisehearted man,
> in whose heart the Lord had put wisdom, even every
> one whose heart stirred him up to come unto the
> work to do it (Exod. 36:1-2).

The willingness of the people as they came together to work
was apparent to everyone.

And all the wise men, that wrought all the work of the sanctuary, came every man from his work which they made; and they spake unto Moses, saying, The people bring much more than enough for the service of the work, which the Lord commanded to make. And Moses gave commandment, and they caused it to be proclaimed throughout the camp, saying, Let neither man nor woman make any more work for the offering of the sanctuary. So the people were restrained from bringing. For the stuff they had was sufficient for all the work to make it, and too much (Exod. 36:4-7).

That is the way it goes when the Lord moves the hearts of the people. Would it not be wonderful if the Lord would raise up people like this even so far as we are concerned: in our churches, Sunday Schools and on radio programs. How we would want the Lord to move people so they would be willing to do His work! This whole program was concluded with the blessing of the Lord.

And Moses did look upon all the work, and, behold, they had done it as the Lord had commanded, even so had they done it: and Moses blessed them (Exod. 39:43).

In chapter 40 there are specific instructions as to how Moses was to lay out the furniture of the tabernacle: "Thus did Moses: according to all that the Lord commanded him, so did he" (Exod. 40:16). The record makes it clear that all this was not Moses' idea. He did not plan that building and he did not arrange the furniture; the Lord led him step by step. Moses was a well-educated man and a wise man, and some of the workers he directed were expert; but the Lord led them to put their talents to work to get this done. This is clear in chapter 40, verse 16: "Thus did Moses: according to all that the Lord commanded him, so did he." Again in verse 19, the phrase is used ". . . as the Lord commanded Moses"; the same is true in verses 21, 23, 25, 27, 29, and 32. Isn't that amazing? Over and over this was recorded. They did as they were told to do; they did as God planned they should do.

When the account reports "So Moses finished the work" (Exod. 40:33), it goes on to say, "Then a cloud covered the tent of the congregation" (Exod. 40.34). It is important to note how they had done it. They did as they were told. The record is clear as to how they had built it. They had done all things as the Lord had commanded Moses. The men who worked in there were the very ones God led to that work. Then persons who had put it all together were the very ones whom God had filled their spirits to make them willing. God had given them wisdom to do it, and Moses had led them.

> Then a cloud covered the tent of the congregation, and the glory of the Lord filled the tabernacle. And Moses was not able to enter into the tent of the congregation, because the cloud abode thereon, and the glory of the Lord filled the tabernacle. And when the cloud was taken up from over the tabernacle, the children of Israel went onward in all their journeys: but if the cloud were not taken up, then they journeyed not till the day that it was taken up. For the cloud of the Lord was upon the tabernacle by day, and fire was on it by night, in the sight of all the house of Israel, throughout all their journeys (Exod. 40:34-38).

This is called "the Shekinah Glory." The word "shekinah" means glory of glories, the most glorious thing.

In the New Testament a similar event occurred on the Day of Pentecost when the disciples were gathered together. The dwelling place of the Holy Spirit of God was brought together by the power of God. When those believers gathered together in one place, and everything had been done as it was supposed to be done, with all the people yielded to God as they were supposed to be yielded, trusting in the Lord as they were supposed to trust in the Lord, everything done as He wanted it done after a ten-day prayer meeting, suddenly Almighty God sent the Holy Spirit. The Holy Spirit filled them very much like the Shekinah Glory cloud filled the tabernacle there in the wilderness. God manifested His presence by showing Himself to be there and filling the people with joy because the Lord was with them.

*Chapter 38*

## CONSECRATION OF THE PRIESTS

Did you know that every believer is called to serve the Lord as a priest in the course of his living here upon earth?

"Unto him that loved us, and washed us from our sins in his own blood, and hath made us kings and priests unto God and his Father" (Rev. 1:5-6). Notice particularly that Christ hath made us "kings and priests unto God."

The Gospel reveals the plan of God in salvation. It reveals the fact that not only is a person forgiven, redeemed, and regenerated as a child of God when he believes, but God gives to all believers an assignment, making them kings and priests. As a king I am called to control my personal activities into His will. The king is to be in charge. I am to rule over my body as a king under God. I am to rule over my own spirit as a king unto God. I am to rule over my mind and my heart. I am responsible before God for what I do, for the things I feel, for the way I think about things, and the way I want things. As a priest I am called to offer gifts and sacrifices for sins and to have compassion on the ignorant and on them that are out of the way. Such is my responsibility as a believer.

Just now we shall be thinking about priests. We can learn much from the procedure by which the priests were consecrated in the time of the Exodus of Israel. All of this was set forth by Moses to the people as it is recorded in Exodus 29. In this account we are told about the preparation of certain persons to be priests. Being a priest is an office in which a function is performed. Since God has made believers in Christ both kings and priests, we shall notice with close interest how these servants of God were prepared in the day of Moses and Aaron. Thus we will learn something of the way believers today are prepared for their ministry in their generation.

What service would a believer render today in the sense that he is a priest? By praying for people — for those in his own family, for friends, for people in the church, for all men everywhere. Interceding on behalf of others is the basic function of a priest.

"And this is the thing that thou shalt do unto them to hallow them, to minister unto me in the priest's office" (Exod. 29:1). Certain things were to be done to "hallow" them: to make them "holy," as it were; to prepare them so that they would be fit for the priest's office. The procedure was to begin with a simple act ". . . wash them with water." This was a ceremonial procedure, to be sure, but it had a real significance. The person was to be washed from the remains or the evidences of sin. They were to stand before God as if they had been washed clean. No sin could be washed off unless it had been confessed. These candidates would then have confessed their sins and forsaken them, which was implied by washing themselves with water. This would indicate that steps had been taken to remove the traces of sins.

"Then shalt thou take the anointing oil, and pour it upon his head, and anoint him" (Exod. 29:7). Anointing was done by pouring oil on the head of any person to be placed in a certain office. When David was called to be king, Samuel anointed him; just as when Saul became king, Samuel anointed him. The anointing was a procedure which indicated that one was to do a certain work. In our day and time believers are anointed by the Holy Spirit of God, and this is the anointing that comes upon us.

Also in this same chapter is revealed that those who were to serve as priests were to be clothed. Certain garments were to be put on them in order to consecrate them, and those garments were unique. There was to be a golden plate across the forehead. On it was inscribed, "Holiness unto the Lord." This could suggest they were to think and plan in terms of being holy. They carried on their shoulders certain structures that were called epaulets — one on each shoulder. There was a precious jewel on each epaulet with the names of six tribes engraved on it. This meant that the priest was to carry the names of six tribes on one shoulder and six tribes on the other shoulder. This would indicate that the priest was to carry the people to God by his power, since the shoulders usually suggest the strength of a man. The priest was also to wear a certain breastplate of gold that had set in it twelve precious stones. On each one of these gems was the name of one of the tribes, which would indicate the priest carried these tribes one by one on his breast, in his love, as he came before God in worship.

There were other things in their attire, but I shall mention only some that I want to bring to your attention. There was a frontispiece, or a bar of gold, across the forehead inscribed with "Holiness unto the Lord"; epaulets on their shoulders carrying the names of six tribes on one, six tribes on the other; also a breastplate with twelve precious stones each engraven with the name of one tribe. Thus the priest was to come into the presence of God aware of the purpose of God to bring His people unto Himself in His holiness, carrying the tribes before God in his strength (the epaulets) and in his love (the breastplate).

In preparing themselves for their service these priests were to bring a sin offering (Exod. 29:14). Why? Because they had sinned and they would continue to sin. They were sinful persons, even as you and I. If we are going to serve God in praying for other people, one of the things we will need to keep in mind is that we must constantly confess our sins to God. The priests were also to bring a burnt offering (Exod. 29:18). The use of the burnt offering indicated total consecration. Nothing was to be left out of their commitment. They were to be completely, totally committed to this task. They were to come confessing their sins and yielding themselves completely unto God. (See pp. 133-34.) "And whatsoever ye do in word or deed, do all in the name of the Lord Jesus." The blood on the great toe of the right foot indicated that the priest should walk in the way of God's will.

This has a profound message for the believer today. It is proper to think of the blood as the death of the Lord Jesus Christ and so as believers go forward doing their service in worshiping God and in serving Him by praying for other people, they have their blood-marked ears open to the call of God, their blood-marked hands ready to do His work, and their blood-marked feet ready to walk in His ways, in a blood-marked walk.

The priests also were given a wave offering. There was put into their hands a certain offering that they were to bring into the presence of God and wave back and forth before God — "We bring Thee but Thine own." When all such preparation was completed, the Scriptures record this Word of God:

> And I will sanctify the tabernacle of the congregation, and the altar: I will sanctify also both Aaron and his sons, to minister to me in the priest's office. And I will dwell among the children of Israel, and will be their God. And they shall know that I am the Lord their God, that brought them forth out of the land of Egypt, that I may dwell among them: I am the Lord their God (Exod. 29:44-46).

How does all of this apply to us? Believers in the Lord Jesus Christ are given a certain commission. Each of us is to act like a king in control of those things that are under our hands, and we are to serve as priests for other people and have compassion on those who are out of the way. We are to come before God, listening to Him, carrying these persons on our shoulders and on our breasts with our strength and with our affection, bringing them into the presence of God that they might be blessed. If we will do that, God will bless us that we will know He is our God and that He is taking care of us.

## Chapter 39

## NADAB AND ABIHU

Can you understand that the manner in which a person comes to God when he is worshiping Him really matters?

To have the blessing of God it is necessary that a person obey His will. It is essential that the believer think about God when he is worshiping Him. Usually the worshiping of God involves certain procedures in which the believer shares certain activities which have been endorsed as acceptable to God. For instance, God has set aside one day in seven to worship Him. This is the day we commonly call the Lord's Day. In the Ten Words God gave to Moses, one of them was "Honor the Sabbath Day. Keep it holy." Also, by way of helping themselves in this matter of coming to God, believers usually have a special place, a building sometimes called a church building, which is used as a sanctuary where people meet to worship God.

Believers usually have an order of service in which they undertake to make sure there is praise to God, thanksgiving to God; and there is petition in which they ask God for blessing. They hear the Word of God in the reading of the Scripture, and meditation is included in the sermon. They teach their children to be reverent in the church building, to be present at the church services, to be humble when they are in the house of God, and to be penitent when they come to worship and to believe, to trust God.

As the children of Israel were traveling across the desert they were given a ritual of worship that was to be led by the priest. They were, after all, just human beings, and if as human beings they intended to look to God, how would they worship Him? What would they do? Some activity needed to be outlined. The children of Israel had such activity outlined for them by Moses, who instructed them as to how this was to be done. Moses designated Aaron and his sons to lead the people through this activity, just as today worshipers generally look to the minister to demonstrate the proper attitudes and activities of worship.

In Leviticus 10 there is a very solemn warning about this matter of worship routines.

> And Nadab and Abihu, the sons of Aaron, took either of them his censer, and put fire therein, and put incense thereon, and offered strange fire before the Lord, which he commanded them not (Lev. 10:1).

They did something else in addition to what they had been told to do. They came into the presence of God to worship Him, but they acted improperly. They acted in their own way rather than in the way which the Lord had commanded, and thus they offered "strange fire before the Lord."

> And there went out fire from the Lord, and devoured them, and they died before the Lord (Lev. 10:2).

It happened just exactly as this simple account reads. These disobedient servants were promptly destroyed.

In some incidents in the Old Testament where there was a record that for the first time some servant did something wrong there was a severe judgment from God. It was as if God were saying, "That is what I think about that." It did not happen that way in every case because God is merciful and gracious; and He remembers that man is but dust. So He often allowed many things to happen that were in disobedience, without such severe complete judgment. There was a similar occurrence recorded in the New Testament when Ananias and Sapphira came into the presence of God, offering a certain gift to the early church. They pretended their gift was all the money they had received from the sale of a piece of property, but it was not. Peter judged them on the spot for lying. He told them that as long as they had the money they could have kept it since it was their own, but when they came into the presence of God they should have been honest about their claim. They dropped dead.

It does not follow that all liars in the church will drop dead, but this first occurrence showed what God thinks when someone lies to Him in His presence. This is a vivid demonstration of how God thinks about an offering being made to Him which is "strange" and unauthorized, being offered in a way that He did not command.

Moses explained what happened:

> Then Moses said unto Aaron, This is it that the Lord spake, saying, I will be sanctified in them that come nigh me, and before all the people I will be glorified (Lev. 10:3).

This was a way of saying, "This is what God meant when He said 'I am going to be treated with reverence. People coming into my presence must do so my way, in the way I say. This is an illustration and an example of what will happen when they do not.'" Later in that chapter it is written that others were detailed to carry the bodies out of the camp away from the people to the community dump heap. Then Moses gave them these instructions, "Uncover not your heads, neither rend your clothes," which is a way of saying, "Don't put on mourning attire, do not grieve or make public exhibition of the fact that you are mourning over the death of these men."

Is there any clue as to why Nadab and Abihu did this foolish thing? This is implied in the account,

> And the Lord spake unto Aaron, saying, Do not drink wine nor strong drink, thou, nor thy sons with thee, when ye go into the tabernacle of the congregation, lest ye die (Lev. 10:8-9).

It seems that Nadab and Abihu had taken strong drink and were drunk when they offered this "strange fire." It is also written why God rejected it, "that ye may put difference between holy and unholy, and between unclean and clean" (Lev. 10:10).

One of the wonderful New Testament doctrines is that every believer is a priest unto God, so that every believing person on earth has his commission to act on behalf of other people. They are to pray for and have compassion for other people; they are to lead other people in the worship

of God. Believers on earth are the ones from whom unbelievers learn. Their conduct as they go among people should
include nothing that is careless. They may not act in ways
that would necessarily be considered popular. In fact, they
may not act just as they please; everything they do must
be under control. There must be nothing willful in their
behavior; they will be guided in what they do. They must
be very careful they do not act on their own. They must
seek to serve God.

Any time a believer thinks about approaching and talking
to God he should have in mind this one thing: Nadab and
Abihu came into the regular worship service to go about
their worship activity, but they went about it in a wrong
way. They conducted themselves according to their own
ideas, and this proved to be disastrous. It is a very solemn
fact that servants who actually are called to serve Him can
make the dreadful mistake of acting as they please, so that
they will be judged unfit in the sight of God.

## Chapter 40

## LAWS FOR HOLINESS

Can you see the importance of a believer acting in complete obedience to the guidance of God?

"To make a difference between the unclean and the clean" are the words found in Leviticus 11:47. These words are repeated over and over again in Leviticus when Moses outlined certain instructions to the people in order to differentiate the clean and the unclean. That which is clean is acceptable to God; that which is unclean is unacceptable to God. It is the essence of intelligence to know the difference.

After the tragic folly of Nahab and Abihu that we noted in our last study, Moses detailed instructions for conduct for the people of Israel. He demonstrated in them, for us and for all time, that a very important aspect of living by faith is the exercise of discrimination. Some things are right; some are wrong. Some things are good; some are bad. Some things are clean; some are unclean. God has set forth standardizations of His expectations which are to be found in the Ten Commandments. God is permanently as He is. Jesus Christ is the same yesterday, today, and forever. There are some things absolutely acceptable to God and other things are absolutely not acceptable to Him. Men may not like it. The mind of man may flinch when he faces this fact, but it is true nonetheless. Men may not recognize the things that are right or wrong, but they will be judged in the sight of God according to whether they want to do the right thing or the wrong thing.

In the Garden of Eden the forbidden fruit was within reach of Adam. He was given a simple command: Don't eat of it. That was all: no argument, no explanation. Eating that fruit was out of line — forbidden. But it should be noted that God left Adam within reach of it. Adam could be impressed that it looked good, it would taste good, and he could be impressed with the idea that if he ate of that fruit he would be wise. God allowed all those things to be before him, but He had given Adam the simple commandment: Do not eat of that tree. Adam did eat, and in that sin not only he fell, but all mankind fell in him.

One thing is required of man — that he obey God. What does this mean so far as man is concerned? It means he cannot do as he pleases. If there is any one sure thing true about this universe in which we live, it is that we cannot do as we would like to do. Every now and again we come to a precipice, and if we fall off we will get hurt. There are things in this world of such a nature that in themselves they would kill us, and we are right in the middle of all these things. How can we learn obedience to God? By God's requiring that man refrain from taking what is within reach, that he restrain himself so that he will not take the forbidden fruit.

We read the sad story about Nadab and Abihu, who did not restrain themselves. They allowed themselves license to do as they pleased. It resulted in their destruction. Sometimes the forbidden is obviously harmful and hurtful, but not always. Sometimes that which is forbidden can look attractive, as it did in the Garden of Eden. Some may wonder if we are not allowed more freedom in the New Testament. There the commandment is: deny thyself. "If any man will come after me let him deny himself." What does that mean? I cannot do as I please. No! That is what it means — no!

In order to teach Israel this principle of self-restraint, Moses used the concept of "clean and unclean." In the book of Leviticus, just after the incident when Nadab and Abihu made their fatal mistake that resulted in their destruction, Moses wrote twelve chapters (from chapter 11 through chapter 22) containing varied instructions to guide the children of Israel specifically about what was right and what was wrong. They were to do the things that would promote "holiness." We can feel its importance when we read in Hebrews 12:14 "without which no man shall see the Lord."

What is this holiness? Is it a description of moral virtue? No, but it is a description of personal commitment. "Holiness" comes from the English word "whole"; and it means wholeness, which is to say, one hundred percent, total commitment, no reservation. To spell this out in terms of conduct, Moses wrote the twelve chapters of instruction. We do not spell out specifics in the same way because we count on the Holy Spirit. The Holy Spirit shows to believers the will of God about each individual matter. As we look at these chapters, we should keep in mind that this was for another culture, at another time; but even so they will have elements in them that are suggestive to us.

Moses gave specific instructions how they should be careful about their food. They were not to eat everything, only what was authorized. This has significance for guidance today. The dietary rules ascribed to Moses are considered to be hygienically sound by the medical profession. But the principle involved need not be limited merely to physical food. In the matter of mental food: personal thinking; so far as the books we read, the pictures we see, the things we talk about are concerned, great care should be exercised about those things.

Moses also discussed the matter of infection. Caution was to be exercised when detecting anything that looked like an infection. There was an elaborate procedure to follow for cleansing, which meant that a person should be careful about getting a disease and about spreading it. This can also be significant in guiding our thoughts. We should be very careful how we associate with other people, lest we pick up defiling ideas.

In the worship of God the children of Israel were to be sensitive about their sins: they were to seek to make atonement. They were to get themselves right with God by humbly confessing their sins and bringing in their sacrifices, as believers now do when they plead the death of the Lord Jesus Christ on their behalf. They were to avoid strange, pagan ideas and practices.

In the matter of morals they were specifically instructed.

They were to be absolutely sure they carried out the spirit of the Ten Commandments in honoring their parents and in keeping the Sabbath Day. Their offerings to God were to be willingly made. They were to be charitable to the poor and honest in their dealings with each other. They were not to be tale bearers, nor to gossip about one another. They were to avoid the occult, dealing with spirits, and so on. They were to honor old age.

Moses touched upon many other things, any one of which would be even more significant to us today because we have the Holy Spirit of God to show us the things that would be acceptable to God and those not acceptable. The principle lesson for believers to learn from this portion of Scripture is that believers should not do as they please because they might please to do wrong. Believers should be careful to control themselves, to restrain themselves that they might accept that which is pleasing in the sight of God and so receive the blessing of God.

## Chapter 41

## ORDER IN MARCH

Can you understand that if a person were obedient to God he would take his place in relation to others?

"In the first place went the standard of the camp of the children of Judah" (Num. 10:14). This is a description of the beginning of their journey as the Israelites set out across the desert. There is much truth implied in the arrangements which set up the order of march.

It is natural to want to be free. This is the infant's style. This is the way a baby acts. If there is any one thing that marks the activity of a baby it is random activity. The baby goes in all directions. Out of this free choice emerges the individual that becomes the person. But spontaneous, uncontrolled license to do as a person pleases will never produce anything of value or of merit. When anyone is acting as he pleases we can be sure that he is sinning. Such conduct will never produce anything of value, and more importantly, such conduct is not at all like Christ.

Jesus of Nazareth said, "I do nothing of myself. My Father worketh hitherto and I work." In yet another place He said, "I do all things to please my Father." This is the big difference between Adam, the first man, and Christ, the Lord from heaven. In the case of Adam, the center of his control, the point toward which his thinking was oriented, was himself; and in the case of Christ Jesus the point toward which He was oriented was His Father. He did nothing apart from His Father, just as Adam did what suited him. This helps us to understand about salvation, which is the work of God in believers, that God is calling the children of Adam to become His children in Christ Jesus.

The work of God which we call salvation in believers

174

through Christ Jesus is marked by the demand for obedience on the part of the believer to a plan that God has for him. God is a God of order, not confusion. When Moses undertook the task of training the children of Israel in the ways of God, he introduced into their consciousness patterns of order. We have been noting how he drilled them in the concept of clean and unclean so far as their personal conduct was concerned. This would apply to their individual responses, their personal action. This is right and that is wrong. This will do and that won't do. This is clean and that is unclean. All of these things were drilled into them for personal conduct, but Moses also arranged for the children of Israel to act in concert when all would move together. He instructed them how to do in joint action.

The children of Israel were divided into tribes. We call them "the twelve tribes of Israel," although there were actually thirteen. In the list of the twelve tribes there is no mention of Joseph, but there are named Ephraim and Manasseh, sons of Joseph. In the list of tribes the Levites are not mentioned. Why? They were called to serve the tabernacle so that they gave themselves to the service of the Lord, in the matter of leading the religious exercises around the tabernacle. They received no land for their sustenance, although the twelve tribes, which included Ephraim and Manasseh, each received portions of land. The Levites were supported by the tithes of the others.

Each of the twelve tribes was allotted its place in the camp. Moses arranged that any time they were camped they were to settle in this fashion: in the center the tabernacle was set up and inside the tabernacle and in the courtyard the Ark and various articles of furniture were placed. The twelve tribes were arranged not in a circle but three tribes to the north, three tribes on the east, three tribes on the south, and three tribes on the west. The arrangement was always the same. This introduced order into their affairs as each tribe took the place that was given to it. When they began marching three tribes would lead off, after which the Levites would bring the tabernacle, then three tribes would follow them, then one family of Levites would bring the Ark, after which were three more tribes.

Some distance in the rear was a fourth set of three tribes, the rear guard, who defended the people in the event of an attack from the rear. They always traveled in this same way, in this same order. This required knowledge of the will of God and obedience.

For any human being to be willing to accept such specific arrangement in obedience requires humility. Whenever they camped, this was the way they camped; whenever they rose to march, this was the way they marched. This reflects another characteristic that should be mentioned, namely, consistency. These three characteristics, obedience, humility, and consistency, are required today among believers. It is instructive to see how all this was pictured for us in the experience of Israel when they were brought out of Egypt into the land of Canaan. Paul wrote that these things happened to them for ensamples and "they are written for our learning upon whom the ends of the world have come." Peter referred to those who believe in the Lord Jesus Christ as "living stones" in the temple. This is true about a stone in the wall: such a stone has its place in the wall and it is to be there to fill that place. This seems to be the idea that is conveyed in the New Testament about believers. Each has his place in the body of Christ and each is to fill the place to which he is assigned.

If we should ask ourselves, "Is this important for believers in Christ?" we can be assured that it is. Believers are to yield to the Spirit within them, and the Spirit within them will prompt each to accept the place assigned to him and to fill it to the best of his ability.

## Chapter 42

## SENDING OF THE SPIES

Can you see how taking time to study an idea may simply be a way to avoid doing anything about it?

"Whatsoever thy hand findeth to do, do it with all thy might." These words are for believers. In our study of the Exodus as we note the journeys of Israel we are going over new ground and this is how it will be in salvation as the believer lives in the will of God. The believer has guidance and he has promises. The promises he has are such that he can afford to believe that he is always exactly where the Lord wants him to be, facing the situation God has in mind for him. For this reason the believer should act immediately on what is before him just as he sees it. That is his business and this is the meaning of the above verse in the Scriptures.

In the salvation work of God much is done by the Lord Himself and for this believers should praise Him. They should rejoice in the knowledge that all is of the Lord. Much that is done through Christ, in Christ, by Christ is so wonderful it is beyond anything we could ask or think. I have heard some say, "God will do everything. You don't have to worry, He will do everything." And this is true. But it is important to remember that the third and final phase of salvation is expressed in the shortest word: "Go." The first word is "Come," the second word is "Abide." It is important to remember this. It is wonderful to recall all that begins with "Come," and the promises that are involved. It is important and often a neglected truth that when the believer has come, he must "abide." I am afraid many come and after they have come, they go home to dinner. They do what they did before. This is not good enough. When a person comes, he is to abide. When he has turned to the Lord he must draw nigh unto Him and walk with Him.

The essential thing to remember about this whole process is that the salvation work is not complete unless and until the believer "goes." The Bible has been kept for willing souls. Believers in Christ believe in Bible study. But the study of Scriptures can be missed. People who want to read and study the Bible need only to consider the difficulties and frustrations encountered when they set out to study. There are other things to do, other books to read, and other matters to attend to. Also, when we actually get into the study of the Bible we find it was originally written in the Old Testament in Hebrew mostly, and in the New Testament in Greek. It is easy to feel there is so much involved which we do not understand; it is easy to become discouraged.

The believer often may settle for a delayed reaction. He may say, "Some day I will do this. When I get around to it, I will do this." All of which will be just an alibi. The deed will never be done. He needs to read, that is all. He only needs to read and to study and to think and pray. There is talk about church visitation, and it would be wonderful if believers would go out and witness in their community. It would not be just a matter of building up the church; it actually would be a fruitful thing to do. Often a believer may feel that he does not know what to do. The man he wants to talk to may have negative feelings and that thought may well scare him. He may be inclined to ask someone to study the situation and give him suggestions; he may possibly try to appraise the whole situation, asking is it worthwhile? Then he may possibly try to recommend what should be done. What I am pointing out is this: we may have classes, visitation projects, prayer meetings about visitation, and we can actually organize ourselves completely, but unless we get out and do it, nothing is going to happen. We can fool ourselves into thinking we did something when actually we only went through the motions. There is a tendency in all of us to delay in actually doing anything.

We may talk about praying in the same way. We may

consider the schedule we have and see that it appears we don't have time for praying: we are preoccupied with other necessary things. And we may not have the mind for it. We will appoint a committee to canvas the situation whether we should pray: to evalute, to propose, to recommend what we should pray for, but we don't pray. That committee business lulls us into thinking we are doing something about it.

The Israelites had a certain goal in mind for years and they were now, at the point where we are studying, on the verge of entering into the land of Canaan. Moses had given them a clear commission: "Go in and possess. Make it your own. You have been led by the hand until here. Now take hold and go in." Until now they had not been challenged to undertake anything on their own. They had been slaves and were like children. They had not been assigned any specific task, and there was an unknown risk involved in going ahead. Going into this strange country, among strange people, was dangerous. They intended to do it of course, but they were not really aware of how much it would mean. As a result they did not get it done. Since there was peril involved it was easy for them to delay a definite decision that they might have time to give the whole project adequate consideration. When the spies brought back a divided judgment about the land saying it was worthwhile but there were great difficulties, the people felt very weak and the majority favored no action.

Of course they had sent the spies. They had considered the matter, and so could easily have been led into thinking they were paying attention to it; but what they were actually doing was avoiding doing anything definite.

> For some, when they had heard, did provoke: howbeit not all that came out of Egypt by Moses. But with whom was he grieved forty years? was it not with them that had sinned, whose carcases fell in the wilderness? And to whom sware he that they should not enter into his rest, but to them that believed not? So we see that they could not enter in because of unbelief (Heb. 3:16-19).

I appreciate the fact that they were guilty of unbelief but we are noting this unbelief was covered over, in a sense, by the sending of the spies. This was a case of just going around the bush to do nothing. They made all their plans but did nothing. This can happen with us in our Bible study. We can take so much time in preparation that we do not have any time left for the study itself.

This action by Israel was called provoking God. God is not provoked when a sinner is an unbeliever. That is natural. It does not provoke God when an unbeliever turns away. That is what is to be expected. But it is provoking to God when someone has been shown and has been blessed, and then delays and lets the matter stand still, when he knows right well he should be going forward. When the believer knows what to do and does not do it, this is provoking to God.

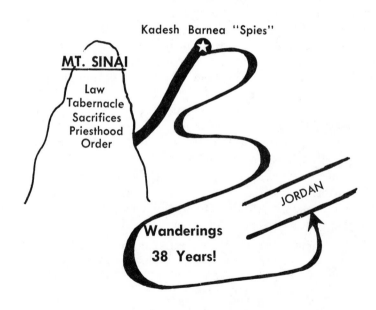

**KADESH BARNEA**

## Chapter 43

## MINORITY REPORT

Do you realize that in a debatable issue, when something has been placed before a group of people and has been discussed pro and con, so they finally vote on it, sometimes the minority may be right?

This world is so uncertain, no matter how hard we may plan, or how carefully we may try to understand everything, it is always easy to make a mistake. Things could turn out differently from our expectations and because of this it is probably natural that there should be real differences of opinion as to what should be done. Some will think we should proceed along one line and others will think we should not do anything. Various ideas will be set forth. When a believer looks ahead there is always the possibility that God may take a hand in his affairs. The believer knows that God is watching over him, and he is hoping and expecting and praying that God will help him. In deciding what to do on the basis of what is going to happen, what he thinks God will do makes a big difference. If he thinks God will not change the course of events, he will decide in a natural way what to do. If he thinks God will affect the local situation so that God will work things out to do His will, he will then try to make his decision on a spiritual basis.

Generally speaking, most people do not expect God to do anything about what they are facing. They talk as if God were in control and, in a sense, deep down in their hearts they may think God is in control, and they may somehow hope that God will work things out well; however, when we come right down to it, and they are actually facing a practical situation, they do not think God will do anything about this situation today. There are few who expect God will do something about their problem today.

But would God do something because they asked Him? Many will get out of that dilemma one way or another. They may say, "He will do something if it is wise, or if it suits Him." But will He act in answer to prayer? That is where unbelief shows up. The true believers often act differently because they think God will answer prayer. They not only think God can, but they think God intends to, and in any given situation they will try and figure out the will of God, and they will count on that in making their own plans and decisions for conduct.

This was demonstrated in the Exodus of Israel in a definite way at the time the Israelites passed through the desert and reached Kadesh-Barnea. At this point they did not feel able to go into the land, although Moses had told them to go in. They decided to send a committee to investigate. There were three things they were to study: first, is the land worthwhile? Would it be a good idea to try to enter? Should they commit themselves to God and go into this project? Second, if they decided to go, would there be difficulties? Would they run into any kind of trouble? Third, if they ran into trouble would it be such as they could handle?

The twelve spies went into the land, and after making a study they came back to report. "Is it worthwhile?" They were unanimous — twelve to nothing — yes! Very much worthwhile. The land was fertile. "Are there difficulties?" Oh, yes. There were high-walled cities that were like forts and there were soldiers well equipped who looked like giants. There were no explosives in those days. To attack such walls they might use a device called a battering ram, which was a big log used to batter against a wall and break it down. Another device was a catapult that would hurl stones like rocks which could be thrown into a city or against a wall. Both of these contraptions took considerable ingenuity and skill as well as materials to build, and these children of Israel had been in the wilderness for many years where they had no opportunity to secure that kind of equipment. When they thought of going up against high-walled cities without equipment they said, "We can't do it." To the third question, "Can we do it?" ten said "No," two of them Joshua and Caleb, said, "It can be done."

No doubt Joshua and Caleb recognized the difficulties as well as the others, but they gave utterance to this famous phrase, "If God be for us, who can be against us? We are well able to take the land with the help of God." These two were men of faith and they would have gone forward trusting in God; but the majority were unbelievers. In this case the majority ruled, but the majority was not right. Believers may face the challenge of drawing nigh unto the Lord wherever they may happen to be. Can they do this? Are they able to plan their affairs in such a way that they can take time for Bible study, for a ministry of prayer? Can they establish a schedule of public fellowship with other believers? Can they make their plans to go to church regularly? When there are special prayer meetings, will they go? If a special effort is being made to help people who are in need, will they help? In such matters as this the challenge arises.

How about money? Shall the believer give to the poor? When he plans a life of obedience to the Lord will he be diligent about these things? about witnessing to others? about attendance at church services?

There will be a real temptation to say "All that is very fine to talk about but it cannot be done in this day and time." To be sure, such difficulties are great and, left to themselves, believers may not be able to do it, but "our God shall fight for us." Believers can be sure that if they go forward trusting in Him, they can expect Him to bring things to pass in His blessing.

## Chapter 44

## CONSEQUENCES OF UNBELIEF

Has it ever occurred to you that when a believer does not obey God in a specific situation, he is in danger of losing what progress he has already made?

Salvation is something that begins in us here in this world, where there are moving, changing situations. So far as the believer is concerned, he is very much like a fish swimming in a swiftly flowing river. If you should see a fish lurking in the shadow of a rock in a swiftly flowing river, that fish might seem to be perfectly still, but the truth is that if it were not wiggling and swimming some it would be swept downstream. The fish will have to do a certain amount of swimming to stay in the same place. In just that way, every believer has to do a certain amount of "swimming" to stay close to the Lord. Just as it is true that if the fish does not swim against the current it will be swept away; so it is true that if the believer does not exercise his faith against the trends of the times, he will be swept away from fellowship with the Lord.

When Jesus of Nazareth was here He taught a parable to His disciples that we commonly call the Parable of the Talents. It has in it a sober message. One servant was given ten talents, another servant was given five talents, and a third servant was given one talent. When the master returned he found that the man who had ten talents to start with had won ten more. The master said, "Well done, thou good and faithful servant: thou hast been faithful over a few things, I will make thee ruler over many things" (Matt. 25:21). The servant who had five talents also went out and earned that many more. He received the same commendation. When the master came to the servant who had received one talent this servant said in effect, "I knew you were a hard taskmaster and I didn't want to run the risk of losing what I had so I buried it. Here is your talent." But the master answered, "Thou wicked and slothful servant, thou knowest that I reap where I sowed not, but you have been lazy and that is wicked." Then he said to his other servants, "Take therefore the talent from him, and give it unto him which hath ten talents . . . And cast ye the unprofitable servant into outer darkness." This may seem very stern. But the man who earned nothing was to lose all he had. He had not been true to his trust.

This is true in salvation. Through the Gospel the soul is called into communion with God, and progress toward God will take place in one crisis after another. It seldom takes place in a smooth, steady rise. Usually we pass through one crisis after another, and in each we make some decision that will bring us closer to God. It may be that each crisis involves some risk, but if it should be that the soul feels obedience to God would be too risky so that he is not willing to go ahead, then that soul will deteriorate in relationship with God.

All this was demonstrated in the Exodus of Israel. In our study so far we have learned how the Hebrews, when they reached Kadesh-Barnea, were on the threshold of the promised land, but they failed to go in. When they heard then that they were to go back into the desert, they did not want to do that. They decided to risk an attack in their own strength, but were defeated and were forced to turn back. For thirty-eight years they were doomed to live in the desert.

Yet there are some amazing facts to note. Even though they did not go into the land as they had been instructed to do, the manna came down every day. They were not faithful but God was faithful. And always the Rock that followed them was Christ. Thus the water they required and the necessary items for living were provided by the grace of God that they might live. This was wonderful. The manna continued every morning and the cloud and the fire by day and by night were there to lead them.

Thus they were sustained and they were protected. But they were unhappy. This is the consequence of unbelief. They were distressed. They had no joy because they were not in fellowship with the Lord. They were not in communion with Him.

Thus we can see how the result of unbelief is lingering, persistent distress. This is impressed upon us as we are noting the experiences of the Israelites as they were going through the Exodus. We may well be thinking: Lord, keep us from such a mistake. Help us to go forward with Thee at all times and when we reach the spot where we don't know for sure how it can be done, give us the grace in our hearts to seek Thy blessing, that we may always have Thee watching over us. For Thy name's sake we ask it. Amen.

# Chapter 45

## MURMURING

Can you understand that discontent in the heart is actually grounded in selfishness and vanity?

> And when the people complained, it displeased the Lord: and the Lord heard it; and his anger was kindled; and the fire of the Lord burnt among them, and consumed them that were in the uttermost parts of the camp. And the people cried unto Moses; and when Moses prayed unto the Lord, the fire was quenched (Num. 11:1-2).

That is a simple but profound story. One of the well-known characteristics of all human beings is the tendency to complain. If there is any one thing true about natural man it is that he is going to find fault. Each starts this as a baby. Why do you think a baby cries? Because of something it does not like, something that is uncomfortable. It is always easy and natural to criticize folks. We cry because of our discomfort, we object because of our unwillingness to do a certain thing. The average two-year-old has one normal response when called. The mother calls, "Mary"; the child will say, "No." When she calls that boy "Tom," he will naturally say, "No." That is the first characteristic response of any child, regardless. Later on, when the child learns that there are variations in proceedings and so on, he tends to do the same thing: questioning the route on which he is traveling, complaining about certain procedures, finding fault with management, and so on. There conditions are normal and human; they exist everywhere.

We can learn something about the significance of this by noticing what happened to Israel. Although these were the people of God who had been greatly blessed, and although

God had led them and promised them certain things, we find that generally their response was as it is written in Numbers 11:1-2. This was the normal pattern: complaint, then trouble. Their complaining displeased the Lord and He sent a plague. Then the people asked Moses to intercede for them. Moses prayed for them, and then God spared them. This happened over and over again.

The people began to desire certain things. When the children of Israel left the land of Egypt there were many Egyptians who came along with them. These were not really believers in God, and after they were out on the desert for awhile the record is:

> And the mixed multitude that was among them fell a lusting: and the children of Israel also wept again, and said, Who shall give us flesh to eat? We remember the fish, which we did eat in Egypt freely: the cucumbers, and the melons, and the leeks, and the onions, and the garlic: but now our soul is dried away: there is nothing at all, beside this manna, before our eyes. And the manna was as coriander seed, and the color thereof as the color of bdellium. And the people went about, and gathered it, and ground it in mills, or beat it in a mortar, and baked it in pans, and made cakes of it: and the taste of it was as the taste of fresh oil. And when the dew fell upon the camp in the night, the manna fell upon it (Num. 11:4-9).

In the course of eating the manna for years it had become tasteless. The people had become tired of it. They remembered the variety of food they had in Egypt and they began wishing for those things.

> Then Moses heard the people weep throughout their families, every man in the door of his tent: and the anger of the Lord was kindled greatly; Moses also was displeased (Num. 11:10).

God heard their complaining. Where did that manna come from? God sent it. Why did they have the manna? God provided it for a living. Yet they are complaining. Just like human beings today. Then we read how Moses prayed to God about it:

> I am not able to bear all this people alone, because
> it is too heavy for me. And if thou deal thus with me,
> kill me, I pray thee, out of hand, if I have found
> favor in thy sight; and let me not see my wretched-
> ness (Num. 11:14-15).

Moses was completely outdone. He had done everything
he could for them, but still they were dissatisfied.

The Lord told Moses to enlist seventy men to help him.
Then the Lord said, ". . . Is the Lord's hand waxed short?
thou shalt see now whether my word shall come to pass
unto thee or not" (Num. 11:23). There followed a mighty
demonstration of God's power.

> And there went forth a wind from the Lord and
> brought quails from the sea, and let them fall by the
> camp, as it were a day's journey on this side, and as
> it were a day's journey on the other side, round about
> the camp, and as it were two cubits high upon the
> face of the earth. And the people stood up all that
> day, and all that night, and all the next day, and they
> gathered the quails: he that gathered least gathered
> ten homers: and they spread them all abroad for
> themselves round about the camp. And while the
> flesh was yet between their teeth, ere it was chewed,
> the wrath of the Lord was kindled against the people,
> and the Lord smote the people with a very great
> plague (Num. 11:31-33).

That is the way it ended. They had cried unto the Lord
for certain results. With those results the Lord gave this
evidence of His displeasure. This sort of thing occurred
over and over again in the thirty-eight years of wandering.
It was unnecessary wandering, and although they were
experiencing only what they deserved, they complained
continually.

"And they journeyed from mount Hor by the way of the
Red Sea, to compass the land of Edom: and the soul of the
people was much discouraged because of the way" (Num.
21:4). The people were nearly forty years older now, but
they were also tired and much discouraged "and the people
spoke against God, and against Moses." That is the way
criticism goes: people start criticizing in discontent, and
before long they criticize the very people who are helping

them. Discouraged persons criticize everybody in the church, then they criticize the Bible, and finally they will criticize God. And that is not good.

In the case of Israel, prayer brought salvation to them in spite of what happened. God had sent serpents among them, but when they prayed earnestly the serpents were taken away, and the people were delivered. That is the way it was all through this period of Israel's history. They were wandering in the desert because they did not go forward when they had the opportunity. Because of their failure they had much trouble, but God kept them alive. Still they became more and more discouraged until finally it seemed that everything was hopeless.

## Chapter 46

## MIRIAM CRITICIZES MOSES

Do you realize that when one person is jealous of another person, everything that second person does seems to be wrong to the first person?

As we study salvation, the work of God, we learn much about believers. This matter of being saved is not something that takes place in a moment. It may begin in less time than that, but it goes for a lifetime. Salvation has to do with God working in the believer to will and to do of His good pleasure. And so it happens that those who are believers have dealings with God day in and day out. When one is born again, although he may be genuinely a child of God, he still has the old man with him. His human nature is still there, and as long as he lives he will experience natural ideas from time to time. Thus the outlook for any believer is a mixed one. Part of the believer is human and part of him is spiritual; often the human element comes to the forefront so naturally as to fool even the believer himself. He does not even realize what is happening.

Cain and Abel were brothers, but when Abel was preferred before Cain the record is that Cain became jealous, so that he began to hate Abel, and eventually he killed him. This was a natural, human course of events. Any time several persons are working together on a project, and one seems to become more prominent than the others, there is the temptation to be jealous. This can and does happen among real believers in churches and families and among friends. It is a serious, sobering thing.

An incident occurred in the history of Israel during the Exodus that shows this truth.

And Miriam and Aaron spake against Moses because

191

of the Ethiopian woman whom he had married: for he had married an Ethiopian woman. And they said, Hath the Lord indeed spoken only by Moses? hath he not spoken also by us? And the Lord heard it (Num. 12:1-2).

They claimed the reason for their discontent was that he had married the Ethiopian woman; but when they talked they revealed their hearts and minds. It seems obvious they were dissatisfied because Moses had authority and because he was the spokesman of God's Word.

(Now the man Moses was very meek, above all the men which were upon the face of the earth.) And the Lord spake suddenly unto Moses, and unto Aaron, and unto Miriam, Come out ye three unto the tabernacle of the congregation. And they three came out (Num. 12:3-4).

There God dealt with them. "And the anger of the Lord was kindled against them; and he departed" (Num. 12:9). They had provoked the Lord.

The record of this incident tells its own story.

And the cloud departed from off the tabernacle; and, behold, Miriam became leprous, white as snow: and Aaron looked upon Miriam, and, behold, she was leprous. And Aaron said unto Moses, Alas, my lord, I beseech thee, lay not the sin upon us, wherein we have done foolishly, and wherein we have sinned. Let her not be as one dead, of whom the flesh is half consumed when he cometh out of his mother's womb. And Moses cried unto the Lord, saying, Heal her now, O God, I beseech thee. And the Lord said unto Moses, If her father had but spit in her face, should she not be ashamed seven days? let her be shut out from the camp seven days, and after that let her be received in again. And Miriam was shut out from the camp seven days: and the people journeyed not till Miriam was brought in again. And afterward the people removed from Hazeroth, and pitched in the wilderness of Paran (Num. 12:10-16).

Although Miriam and Aaron used Moses' marriage to the Ethiopian woman to criticize him, their jealousy was the basis for their attack. This angered the Lord. Moses had been chosen to do a certain work. His actions had been directed by God. Do you think something like this could happen in a church? Do you think that several officers could be jealous of another to the degree that their contention would affect the whole work of the church?

The people journeyed not until Miriam was brought into the camp again. Both she and Aaron realized they had been at fault and Aaron came to Moses humbly and besought him to pray for them. He said, "I beseech thee, lay not the sin upon us, wherein we have done foolishly, and wherein we have sinned." Moses did pray, "Heal her now, O God, I beseech thee." This should be somewhat a warning to all who are tempted to criticize the leadership of any congregation. To leaders who feel hindered in their work because of jealousy they can expect God will judge the people in their jealousy, and the people will suffer. It is proper for the man who is a leader like Moses to pray for those people that God may spare them. We should always keep this in mind: this kind of contention among the leadership will result in the people's not making any progress. This could happen to a father and a mother in such a way that the children would suffer. It can happen in a church when the officers of the church fall out with each other; then all of the members of the church will suffer. It can happen between the preacher and his session or his deacons, and when contention develops, all the people will suffer. How common this sad tragedy is!

*Chapter 47*

## REBELLION OF KORAH

Do you think that cooperation in the work of the Lord is simply a matter of personal preference and choice?

Opposition to the leadership in the Lord's work can bring disaster. In our study of the children of Israel as they traveled in the Exodus we saw them having experiences that seemed so unnecessary, that were not in the script, so to speak. The incident of the golden calf was utterly unnecessary. The trouble that developed between Miriam and Aaron and Moses was a personal matter — jealousy and criticism of Moses on the part of Miriam and Aaron. We saw how God took a hand in that matter.

And now we shall see another case of rebellion that resulted differently. This, also, did not need to happen. It is called in the Bible "the rebellion of Korah." It brought about a major crisis and a sad fate for many people.

> Now Korah, the son of Izhar, the son of Kohath, the son of Levi, and Dathan and Abiram, the sons of Eliab, and On, the son of Peleth, sons of Reuben, took men: and they rose up before Moses, with certain of the children of Israel, two hundred and fifty princes of the assembly, famous in the congregation, men of renown: and they gathered themselves together against Moses and against Aaron, and said unto them, Ye take too much upon you, seeing all the congregation are holy, every one of them, and the Lord is among them: wherefore then lift ye up yourselves above the congregation of the Lord (Num. 16:1-3)?

This was a direct and open challenge to the authority that Moses had and to the place that God had given to him. When Moses heard of it he fell upon his face because when

194

they began talking this way Moses realized they were talking against God.

> And he spake unto Korah and unto all his company, saying, Even tomorrow the Lord will show who are his, and who is holy; and will cause him to come near unto him: even him whom he hath chosen will he cause to come near unto him. This do; Take you censers, Korah, and all his company; and put fire therein, and put incense in them before the Lord tomorrow: and it shall be that the man whom the Lord doth choose, he shall be holy: ye take too much upon you, ye sons of Levi (Num. 16:5-7).

This was the very accusation Korah and his people made against Moses and Aaron; but here Moses turns it around. Korah and his people had an important place in the work, being Levites, and they had been given work to do with the tabernacle. Moses reminded them of this when he said:

> Seemeth it but a small thing unto you, that the God of Israel hath separated you from the congregation of Israel, to bring you near to himself to do the service of the tabernacle of the Lord, and to stand before the congregation to minister unto them? And he hath brought thee near to him, and all thy brethren the sons of Levi with thee: and seek ye the priesthood also? For which cause both thou and all thy company are gathered together against the Lord: and what is Aaron, that ye murmur against him (Num. 16:9-11)?

Moses tried to help these rebels to see the folly of their attitude by saying about himself and Aaron, "Do you think we chose this? Do you think we are responsible?"

> And Moses sent to call Dathan and Abiram, the sons of Eliab: which said, We will not come up: is it a small thing that thou hast brought us up out of a land that floweth with milk and honey, to kill us in the wilderness, except thou make thyself altogether a prince over us? Moreover thou hast not brought us into a land that floweth with milk and honey, or given us inheritance of fields and vineyards: wilt thou put out the eyes of these men? we will not come up (Num. 16:12-14).

In verse 15 we are told, "Moses was very wroth." These

were important men who had a share of leadership in the congregation. Moses had proposed that they come together to discuss the problem, but when they refused he said unto the Lord, "Respect not thou their offering." When they were finally brought together, the Lord said unto Moses and Aaron, "Separate yourselves from among this congregation, that I may consume them in a moment." In this way the Lord was testing Moses.

> And they fell upon their faces, and said, O God, the God of the spirits of all flesh, shall one man sin, and wilt thou be wroth with all the congregation? (Num. 16:22).

When they were lined up against each other, Korah, Dathan, and Abiram were on one side with their wives and sons and the little children, standing in the door of their tent.

> And Moses said, Hereby ye shall know that the Lord hath sent me to do all these works; for I have not done them of mine own mind. If these men die the common death of all men, or if they be visited after the visitation of all men; then the Lord hath not sent me. But if the Lord make a new thing, and the earth open her mouth, and swallow them up, with all that appertain unto them, and they go down quick into the pit; then ye shall understand that these men have provoked the Lord. And it came to pass, as he had made an end of speaking all these words, that the ground clave asunder that was under them: and the earth opened her mouth, and swallowed them up, and their houses, and all the men that appertained unto Korah, and all their goods. They, and all that appertained to them, went down alive into the pit, and the earth closed upon them: and they perished from among the congregation. And all Israel that were round about them fled at the cry of them: for they said, Lest the earth swallow us up also. And there came out a fire from the Lord, and consumed the two hundred and fifty men that offered incense (Num. 16:28-35).

This was a terrible thing, and it shocked the whole nation.

> But on the morrow all the congregation of the children of Israel murmured against Moses and against

Aaron, saying, Ye have killed the people of the Lord (Num. 16:41).

Thus they blamed Moses for what had happened.

And the Lord spake unto Moses, saying, Get you up from among this congregation, that I may consume them as in a moment. And they fell upon their faces. And Moses said unto Aaron, Take a censer, and put fire therein from off the altar, and put on incense, and go quickly unto the congregation, and make an atonement for them: for there is wrath gone out from the Lord; the plague is begun. And Aaron took as Moses commanded, and ran into the midst of the congregation; and, behold, the plague was begun among the people: and he put on incense, and made an atonement for the people. And he stood between the dead and the living; and the plague was stayed. Now they that died in the plague were fourteen thousand and seven hundred, beside them that died about the matter of Korah (Num. 16:44-49).

This was a terrible disaster. But how did it start? Because a company of important men who had some authority became jealous of Moses and Aaron and wanted to challenge their leadership, which had been given to them from God. God took a hand and the disaster followed. All of this tells us that the matter of criticizing those in leadership and authority is serious business. We should be very careful not to take it upon ourselves for personal reasons to criticize those who are in the place of leadership.

But let me say to those of you in places of leadership: when it would seem as though the others would be destroyed, note the example from Moses and Aaron. They stepped in and stood between the living and the dead. They stood in the face of that plague and interceded on behalf of those foolish people who had done wrong. There is plain guidance for this day and time. Believers in the Lord who see the foolishness of those who oppose them and suffer because of it, are challenged to pray for their enemies that they may not suffer altogether for their wrongdoing. Such opponents are sinful but they are only human, and God gave His Son to die for them. Believers should have compassion for the lost even when they are foolish and even when they are willful.

## Chapter 48

## DISCIPLINE

Do you realize that in order for power of any kind to work, to actually bring something to pass, it must be under control?

In our study of the whole idea of salvation, we have in mind that it is the work of God, which He works in human beings who believe in Christ Jesus. Just now I want to draw your attention to the fact that this work of God involves certain things that must be done. An apostle Paul testifies:

> And every man that striveth for the mastery is temperate in all things. Now they do it to obtain a corruptible crown; but we an incorruptible. I therefore so run, not as uncertainly; so fight I, not as one that beateth the air: but I keep under my body, and bring it into subjection: lest that by any means, when I have preached to others, I myself should be a castaway (I Cor. 9:25-27).

Paul used a very common and easily recognized truth in physical athletic competition when he said, "I therefore so run, not as uncertainly." He was not going in all directions; he was running like a man running a race. His eye was on the goal. And again, "so fight I, not as one that beateth the air." A fighter uses his hands, his fists and arms but he does not swing in haphazard fashion. He does not thrash the air. He has a purpose in mind, ". . . but I keep under my body, and bring it into subjection." In another place he said, "I buffet my body," which is what he meant by the words "I keep under my body." This was Paul's ambition, to control himself in order that he might get on with his work. This was his purpose, to make his every faculty serve the purpose that he had in heart and mind in obeying the Lord.

Human beings when born into this world are ignorant. They are wayward and their activity is random. They are perverse. They have in them the inward principle of sin which causes them to take the wrong turn again and again. As such they are responsive to the flesh, to the way things look to them from a human point of view. This is all very human. The new birth results in the human being becoming a new creation, a child of God, responsive to the Spirit. And so the believer, the person who has accepted Christ, has in him both flesh, that which he inherited from his father and mother, and spirit, that which he received from God through faith. Both flesh and spirit are active in the one person, yet they are different. The flesh moves along the line of the senses — what I see, what I hear, what I smell, what I taste, and what I touch. The spirit moves along the line of the Word of God. "This is the way, walk ye in it." "I am the Lord thy God. Thou shalt have no other gods before me."

Everything pertaining to spiritual revelation is in the spirit. The spirit is different from the flesh. These have different sources, and often are contrary to each other. The flesh, that with which I was born as a baby, needs to be controlled. It needs to be directed by anyone who seeks to accomplish anything. Even as a baby if I wanted to get my hands on something, I had to control my hands and make them close on what it was I was going to hold. A baby is born with vital energy and often has more strength than we realize. It has motor capacity, but no control of its activities and no direction in its activities. However, the baby learns to control. It learns to bring its hands before itself and to pick up objects. It walks here and there, but this learning goes on with effort. It is hard work for a baby to learn how to control the muscles to exercise even the common functions of living.

In time the child becomes a boy, and the boy becomes a man, to do well, to be actively able to get things done, to strive for mastery requiring self-control. Those acquainted with physical competition know that the competitors train themselves. This is also true in spiritual matters. To bring the physical body under control may involve buffeting, bruising. For a man to enter into a program of training for any physical competition it often involves a grueling period of self-discipline in training exercises where he learns to push himself, to do or not do, to apply his whole energy where it will count most.

When a human being becomes a believer in the Lord Jesus Christ, to bring the spiritual being into the will of God involves for the believer the denial of self, self-crucifixion. This was demonstrated in the affairs of Israel in many ways. Israel was shown over and over how, when they did wrong, certain experiences would follow that were unpleasant. They would be punished. If a mother wanted to train a child not to reach up and interfere with the operation of the kitchen clock, there would be various ways of doing it; but there would be one simple way that child could be trained not to interfere with the clock. When that child put its hands on that clock, someone would slap its fingers. You may say that is physical. But, the fingers were physical to begin with and the clock was physical, so the whole thing was actually a physical operation, and now the child was taught something: that a person does not handle a clock. Nature works that way. Nature fixed it so that the human being would not burn his body. When he puts his finger in the fire, it hurts, and he is warned away from the fire. That is the way nature has of telling you not to do it.

When Israel did not go forward at the time of Kadesh-Barnea Moses told them they would have to go back into the desert. God indicated not one of them would ever enter the land, except Joshua and Caleb. When Miriam criticized Moses she was smitten with leprosy. That was God's way of showing that her conduct was wrong. When Korah and his company rebelled against the leadership of Moses they were all destroyed. From this event all Israel learned a lesson. When the people murmured about eating manna God sent quails, but He also sent a plague. When a man blasphemed the name of God he was arrested, his case considered, and he was stoned to death. A man was found picking up sticks on the Sabbath Day, which he was not supposed to do. The man was accused, then taken out and stoned to death. That was rough treatment — in fact, it was terrible. But it was done to teach them they were not to do such things. When Moses sinned against God he was forbidden to enter into the land. In all these instances it was revealed that God punishes sin.

This principle is included in the Gospel. The Lord Jesus said, "If any man will follow after me, let him deny himself, take up his cross and follow me." The application of this principle was actually described by the Lord, who set out in detail just how this was brought out so far as people were concerned:

> Wherefore if thy hand or thy foot offend thee, cut them off, and cast them from thee: it is better for thee to enter into life halt or maimed, rather than having two hands or two feet to be cast into everlasting fire. And if thine eye offend thee, pluck it out, and cast it from thee: it is better for thee to enter into life with one eye, rather than having two eyes to be cast into hell fire (Matt. 18:8-9).

That is the way the Lord Jesus expressed it. It is illustrated in any orchard when someone prunes the tree, cutting off the unnecessary or dead, superfluous branches so that there may be good fruit. This kind of thing makes us remember how Paul said, "I buffet my body and keep it in subjection." Paul did this in order that he might serve the Lord.

*Chapter 49*

## VICTORY OVER AMORITES

Do you think if a person is truly a believer in Jesus Christ he will ever allow ungodly people to hinder his witness? Do you think a believer should allow ungodly persons to influence him, to alter his testimony, to change what he is doing?

Some seem to think that if a person is a true believer he will never object to anything. He may react something like this, "Even if I don't agree with him, he has a right to his opinion." No doubt many people salve their conscience this way when they do not oppose outspoken error. I would like to ask in what sense any man has a right to teach what is wrong. If you were playing a tune on a violin or a piano, would anyone have a right to pound a bass drum in your ears while that is going on? If you are bringing up your child in a general pattern of polite manners, should you allow crude vulgarity to be practiced in your home?

Let us consider and try to understand the children of Israel in their journey across the wilderness.

> And when king Arad the Canannite, which dwelt in the south, heard tell that Israel came by the way of the spies; then he fought against Israel, and took some of them prisoners. And Israel vowed a vow unto the Lord, and said, If thou wilt indeed deliver this people into my hand, then I will utterly destroy their cities. And the Lord hearkened to the voice of Israel, and delivered up the Canannites; and they utterly destroyed them and their cities: and he called the name of the place Hormah (Num. 21:1-3).

Should there be any protest about that? Would you think that incident belongs in the Old Testament and ought not to be understood in our day and time? Would you say that it was too harsh? Let me tell you something I heard the other day about a fine young woman who is in the hospital. During surgery doctors removed one of her breasts. She paid hundreds of dollars to have that done. Does that sound terrible? At the same time we know of a young child who is in an isolation ward of a hospital, where restrictions are greater than if he were in jail. Does that sound terrible? Now, suppose that child had polio. The restrictions would assure that others would not contract it. If a person had a malignancy of some kind, to remove it might mean that person might live. Surgery may be a means of blessing.

As we consider this situation we should remember that "the cup of the Amorites was already full." We read elsewhere in the Bible that God had dealt with these people. He was the God of the Amorites as well as of the Israelites. Here He guided His own people into this situation and King Arad, of the Canaanites, fought against them and actually took some prisoners. Now what should they do? Should they turn around and go back? Should they allow this ungodly pagan to interrupt them in their program? They talked to God about their situation and they promised Him, "if we are given victory over this man, we will destroy him." This is what happened and this is what they did. Elsewhere in the Bible it is recorded that His people received help from God and won a victory, but then did not destroy the enemy. The result was always bad.

Later the Israelites came to the land of the Amorites and presented a simple humble request for permission to pass through.

> And Israel sent messengers unto Sihon king of the Amorites, saying, Let me pass through thy land: we will not turn into the fields, or into the vineyards; we will not drink of the waters of the well: but we will go along by the king's high way, until we be past thy borders. And Sihon would not suffer Israel to pass through his border: but Sihon gathered all his people together, and went out against Israel into the wilderness: and he came to Jahaz, and fought against Israel. And Israel smote him with the edge of the sword, and possessed his land . . . And Israel took all these cities: and Israel dwelt in all the cities . . .

Thus Israel dwelt in the land of the Amorites (Num. 21:21-31).

Should believers ever admit there are people with whom they should not fraternize? Would such an attitude be too harsh? There are those with whom believers do not agree and they must let that be known. This is never easy to do, and it is especially difficult in a learning situation. If a believer is in a class of philosophy at a university he has to study certain philosophers in that course. Many such writers are pagans. Some of them may present bits of truth. Should the believer concede that the pagan philosopher has an equal right to his thinking as over against what is revealed in the New Testament, in all of the Bible? While the believer may appreciate that author's wisdom and intelligence, at the same time when he compares it with the revelation of God's Word in the Scriptures and finds it different, should he have any hesitation in thinking what the Scriptures reveal, regardless of what the unbelieving author may say?

How much does the believer believe in God? How much does he believe in the Lord Jesus Christ? Does he really believe that Jesus of Nazareth was the Son of God, the Savior of the world? Then that being the case, and with him expecting the Lord to take him to heaven and to glory, should he have any hesitation to compare any man's writing with the words of the Lord and should he have any hesitation to turn to and choose the words of the Lord Jesus Christ as over against those of any man, no matter how famous that man may be?

There are people today who actually object to our missionary program. They say, "Those people have a religion. They have a faith and it suits them. They have a perfect right to it." But I feel that such a view is absolutely wrong on two counts: for one thing all those human beings are God's creatures. He is the one God who is the Maker of every human being. He is the Judge of all the earth, and every human being is going to stand before Him and be judged according to the eternal law of God. The Ten Commandments are going to be applied whether that man heard them or not. That is one fact that cannot be shaken, and so those people should be told how things really stand with God. The other thing is this: the Lord Jesus Christ, while He was here, said, "He that hath seen me hath seen the Father. I am the Way, the Truth, and the Light. No man cometh unto the Father but by me." He was referring to every human being, and indicating the Gospel is for all men.

My good people, each one of us has to face the fact that there are those in the world who do not agree with us, who do not agree with the Scriptures. They do not agree with the Lord Jesus Christ. They have their own ideas. So far as we are concerned, we cannot let such people turn us away from witnessing, from telling the whole wide world that God was in Christ reconciling the world to Himself, that Jesus of Nazareth was the Savior who came into the world to seek and to save the lost, and that whosoever believeth in Him shall not perish but have everlasting life. This is what we must tell the whole world. No matter who says anything else, this is what is true. We believe it, and we must share it with others.

# Chapter 50

## SIN OF BALAAM

Can you believe that it is possible for a person who knows about Jesus Christ to try to lead other people away from Him?

In our study of salvation we are learning much about the devious ways of people, and the cunning, crooked ways of sin. Many have heard of and have an appreciation of God, and yet they do not believe in Him; that is, they have not committed themselves to Him. They are not depending upon God. They have a hope they will be with others, and that God will not destroy all of them. They are wrong. "The soul that sinneth shall die." This is absolutely true.

There are some unbelieving people who appreciate the blessings of the believers. They can even recognize those blessings as coming from God, and they can understand how believers are being blessed because God is blessing them, yet they can be so influenced by some particular consideration in their own hearts they will actually try to keep believers from obeying the Lord. Does that sound strange to you? It sounds so strange I am glad we have a real incident of this sort to study in the Exodus of Israel so that we may follow it through and understand something more about it. In the book of Numbers there is an outstanding example of what we have been thinking about which actually occurred in Israel's experience.

Israel was traveling through the desert. The people were drawing near to the land of Canaan through territory that was occupied by enemies of Israel who did not believe in God. Thus it happened that Israel approached the land of Moab, whose king was Balak.

And the children of Israel set forward, and pitched

in the plains of Moab on this side Jordan by Jericho.
And Balak the son of Zippor saw all that Israel had
done to the Amorites. And Moab was sore afraid of
the people, because they were many: and Moab was
distressed because of the children of Israel (Num.
22:1-3).

The record shows that Balak sent messengers to a prophet
by the name of Balaam. This was a man who knew God. He
could actually receive messages from God which he then
communicated to others. There is no revelation as to what
procedure he followed, whether he did this in an ordinary
exercise of prayer or whether he had some special spiritual
experience. But it was known that he could get messages
from God; Balak was aware of this. The king sent to Balaam
and said in effect, "You are a man of God and God hears you
when you pray. I want you to do something for me. I want
you to ask Almighty God to curse Israel." Balaam sent back
his word of refusal.

And God said unto Balaam, Thou shalt not go with
them; thou shalt not curse the people: for they are
blessed. And Balaam rose up in the morning, and said
unto the princes of Balak, Get you into your land:
for the Lord refuseth to give me leave to go with you.
And the princes of Moab rose up, and they went unto
Balak, and said, Balaam refuseth to come with us
(Num. 22:12-14).

But Balak was not willing to accept this refusal.

And Balak sent yet again princes, more, and more
honorable than they. And they came to Balaam, and
said to him, Thus saith Balak the son of Zippor, Let
nothing, I pray thee, hinder thee from coming unto
me: for I will promote thee unto very great honor,
and I will do whatsoever thou sayest unto me: come
therefore, I pray thee, curse me this people. And
Balaam answered and said unto the servants of Balak,
If Balak would give me his house full of silver and
gold, I cannot go beyond the word of the Lord my
God, to do less or more (Num. 22:15-18).

There is no doubt that so far as Balaam was concerned,
he knew the mind of God. He knew what God would do
and what God would not do, and so he answered in this
fashion:

> Now therefore, I pray you, tarry ye also here this
> night, that I may know what the Lord will say unto
> me more. And God came unto Balaam at night, and
> said unto him, If the men come to call thee, rise up,
> and go with them; but yet the word which I shall say
> unto thee, that shalt thou do. And Balaam rose up in
> the morning, and saddled his ass, and went with the
> princes of Moab (Num. 22:19-21).

Following this is the record of one of the strangest events
of all history. Balaam's ass actually refused to go forward
on this journey and, as we read in the New Testament, the
ass forbade the madness of the prophet, actually speaking to
Balaam and telling him that he was on the wrong road.
However, Balaam insisted on going ahead with his plan.
Balaam said to Balak, "Build me here seven altars"; and
Balak did it.

> And Balaam said unto Balak, Stand by thy burnt
> offering, and I will go: peradventure the Lord will
> come to meet me: and whatsoever he showeth me I
> will tell thee. And he went to an high place (Num.
> 23:3).

This would indicate that he went to worship God. When he
returned he told Balak that it was impossible to do as he
had requested: God would not let him curse His people.
The king did not accept this and he pressed Balaam to find
some way to do it. But Balaam could find no ground on
which to curse Israel. When he said Israel would be blessed,
Balak was furious.

But in Chapter 25 we read that what was impossible for
Balaam to do by spiritual cursing, he was apparently able
to accomplish by advising the Midianites to use guile. Then
follows one of the dark passages of Scripture. The record is
that the children of Israel and the children of Midian
mingled together and committed immorality.

> And Israel abode in Shittim, and the people began to
> commit whoredom with the daughters of Moab. And
> they called the people unto the sacrifices of their
> gods: and the people did eat, and bowed down to
> their gods. And Israel joined himself unto Baal-peor:
> and the anger of the Lord was kindled against Israel
> (Num. 25:1-3).

Isn't that terrible! They found a way of tempting the Israelites through the flesh to commit sin with them and Israel joined themselves unto Baal-peor, a line of religious thinking; so that the anger of the Lord was kindled against Israel.

How often in our day we see sin being committed and we are quite helpless to do anything about it. There is much that godly people are opposed to, yet unable, seemingly, to do anything about. At this point, Phinehas, the grandson of Aaron, saw what was happening; and he did something violent. He rose up from the congregation, took a javelin, and went after the man of Israel into the tent and thrust both of them through — the man and the woman. So the plague was stayed from Israel and those that died in the plague were twenty and four thousand.

It was an awful tragedy that widespread sin could cause so much trouble, but it was stopped right there because one man took it upon himself to take action in condemning that which was wrong. It is the classic strategy of Satan: if he cannot defeat you, he wants to join you. If he is not able to destroy you in an open fight, he will try to get you to come with him on the basis of friendship and so lead you into sin. Some people are actually led into distressing sin just that way.

*Chapter 51*

## COMPROMISE WITH MIDIAN

Can you understand the peril in compromising with ungodly persons because of social relations?

"For Demas hath forsaken me, having loved this present world . . ." wrote the apostle Paul to Timothy (II Tim. 4:10). We are not told a great deal about this man Demas. He is mentioned in one other epistle and, interestingly enough, Paul does not say anything for him one way or another. The will of God calls believers to walk in the way of the Lord, and that is contrary to the prevailing mode of the world. The believer deals with this world on the one hand and with God on the other hand, and they are not alike. The Lord Jesus said that whatsoever is pleasing in the sight of men is an abomination in the sight of the Lord. It is strange how often we overlook that. I suspect many people would be surprised to realize that this is actually recorded in the Bible, ". . . for that which is highly esteemed among men is abomination in the sight of God" (Luke 16:15). The same warning is given by James ". . . know ye not that the friendship of the world is enmity with God?" (James 4:4). This is plain talk, and it leaves us really fearful about ourselves.

In the history of Judah there was a great king by the name of Jehoshaphat. He was a great king, but he had a weakness. He was inclined to fraternize with ungodly men. He made friends with people who were not friends of God.

> And Jehu the son of Hanani the seer went out to meet him, and said to king Jehoshaphat, Shouldest thou help the ungodly, and love them that hate the Lord? therefore is wrath upon thee from before the Lord (II Chron. 19:2).

210

It would be a shock if someone should confront us and ask, "How do you think you are going to get away with it, if you love them that hate the Lord?" That, in effect, is what Jehu said to Jehoshaphat.

All this was experienced by Israel in the Exodus. Perhaps, if we look at one of these incidents in the Exodus of Israel, we can understand more clearly how this unfortunate situation can actually develop. The people of Israel, in their sojourning in the desert, met people who were opposed to them. When they came to King Arad of the Canaanites, he went out to fight against them. The result was that King Arad was destroyed. Shortly thereafter the Israelites came to the country of the Amorites, whose king was Sihon. They asked courteously for the privilege of passing through his country. Sihon refused and gathered his soldiers together to attack Israel, with the result that he was destroyed. Shortly thereafter Og, the king of Bashan, also undertook to oppose Israel and he was destroyed. Later they came to the land of Midian, where Balak was king.

Balak realized that these Israelites were difficult people to resist. All who resisted them had been destroyed. So he adopted a different policy. He acted very friendly. The children of Israel were actually taken in by this seeming friendliness of these ungodly people. They shared with them and as they shared, they began to live with them. The immorality of the Moabites spread into Israel. Not only did they practice immorality but they accepted the ideas of these ungodly people. When we think about that we must not think that these heathen ideas would be obviously wrong. It was actually more as we have it today. No one is likely to ask us to worship an idol of stone or wood. That is not the point today; we will have new ways of looking at things presented, even though they are evil. Today we have people saying, "It is no longer wrong to do this or that," thus leaving the way open for any of us to participate in sinful practices, being lulled into the dangerous state of permissiveness where it can be said "anything goes."

The Lord had given definite instructions to Moses: "Vex the Midianites, and smite them." They were to enter into conflict and resist them. The last task given to Moses to perform on earth was to avenge the children of Israel against the Midianites. Afterwards, ". . . thou shalt be gathered unto thy people."

It is so easy for a child of God to become entangled and so hard to be set free. This is a sober warning for all believers. At no time is the devil so dangerous as when he is friendly, when he is affable. You and I can have in mind that the devil does not appear to anybody with horns and hoofs and tail, spitting fire. He is affable, pleasant, kindly in manner because he is a deceiver. He is a cheat. He is a sneak and he entices people to put their trust in him. This truth can probably be summarized like this: the church is in the world, and that is proper and good; but when the world is in the church, that is disaster. The believing person lives in this world, and that is true; but when the believing person joins this world, it is just too bad! Or it can be put in this way: the ship in the sea is normal and good, but the sea in the ship is tragedy and disaster.

## Chapter 52

## DIVISION OF THE LAND

Do you realize that the normal outlook for a believer is forward and upward?

"If in this life only we have hope in Christ, we are of all men most miserable" (I Cor. 15:19). The mind of a believer is brightened by hope. It is lifted by hope. The heart of a believer is strengthened because of hope. Paul wrote these words:

> For we are saved by hope: but hope that is seen is not hope: for what a man seeth, why doth he yet hope for? But if we hope for that we see not, then do we with patience wait for it (Rom. 8:24-25).

Let me say again, the believer looks forward and upward, which is to say he does not see things the way they are now, but the way they are going to be: not here but there. There may be some benefits here but that is not the point. The believer looks upward into the presence of God, and that is strengthening to him.

It is true that looking back promotes real assurance. In the past is the cross of Calvary, on the horizon of history. Hundreds of years ago Christ Jesus died for sinners and that is still valid and will be forever. That is the basis of assurance with God. A person can actually come into the presence of God with confidence and can stand before Him with expectation, because Christ Jesus died for him. It is not a question of whether he is worth anything. It is not a question of whether what he does is right, or whether he has a good record. It is a question of the Lord Jesus being the Son of God and giving Himself for that soul.

Looking back brings real assurance, but looking up gives real comfort because his Advocate is at the right hand of

God. The believer is not worthy, but this is not the important thing. We should think about the fact that right now in the presence of God, his Lord and Savior is praying for him. At no time does the Lord quit. "The keeper of Israel neither slumbers nor sleeps."

Because I am a believer, looking forward can fill me with joy and gladness. Not because I think I am going to do so much, and not because I think that some day everything will turn out all right, but I have something far surer than that: the blessed hope. In heaven Almighty God through the Lord Jesus Christ has it set up, and those who put their trust in Him will come into His presence to be blessed. I will be there and I do not know how soon. God the Father, the Lord Jesus Christ, and the Holy Spirit right now are doing their part, and because of this I am going to be saved by the grace of God.

If you are a believer in Christ I can't promise you money; I can't promise you health. I *can* promise you that when you get through with this world, and you *will*, you will come into the very presence of God. That is a blessed hope, and it bears thinking about. I can lift up my eyes and look forward to that prospect. I can let the light of the very glory of the city of God shine on my face and into my heart from day to day. That is where He is, and that is where I am going. No wonder Paul could write:

> For which cause we faint not; but though our outward man perish, yet the inward man is renewed day by day. For our light affliction, which is but for a moment, worketh for us a far more exceeding and eternal weight of glory; while we look not at the things which are seen, but at the things which are not seen: for the things which are seen are temporal; but the things which are not seen are eternal (II Cor. 4:16-18).

Isn't that wonderful? Every believer is called to put his heart and mind and his trust in the Lord, looking up at the things which are not seen in this world but which are true.

> Let not your heart be troubled: ye believe in God, believe also in me. In my Father's house are many mansions: if it were not so, I would have told you.

> I go to prepare a place for you. And if I go and pre-
> pare a place for you, I will come again, and receive
> you unto myself; that where I am, there ye may be
> also (John 14:1-3).

These are wonderful words. You will notice something is
missing here in a sense. Nothing is said about my problems.
"You believe in God, believe also in me." Nothing is said
about what is happening this day about what I am doing
now. "In my Father's house are many mansions: if it were
not so, I would have told you. I go to prepare a place for
you." That was the truth to think about. Elsewhere the
Lord Jesus told His disciples "In the world ye shall have
tribulation" (John 16:33). "Man is born unto trouble, as
the sparks fly upward" (Job 5:7). Believers will have
trouble, and their comfort and assurance does not mean that
all their troubles are going to pass away. But they do have
a promise. "But be of good cheer; I have overcome the
world" John 16:33).

It is this glorious prospect of coming into the presence
of God by the power of the Lord Jesus Christ that inspires
obedience and consistent living.

> Behold, what manner of love the Father hath be-
> stowed upon us, that we should be called the sons
> of God: therefore the world knoweth us not, because
> it knew him not. Beloved, now are we the sons of
> God, and it doth not yet appear what we shall be:
> but we know that, when he shall appear, we shall be
> like him; for we shall see him as he is. And every
> man that hath this hope in him purifieth himself,
> even as he is pure (I John 3:1-3).

This aspect of salvation was demonstrated in the Exodus
as the children of Israel came near to the conquest of
Canaan. Moses called all the leaders together before the
campaign for the conquest of the land was finished, and he
authorized the division of the land (Num. 26:52-56). They
had not captured it yet, but they were going to. They had
not yet completed their occupation of the land but they had
a sure hope that the land would be theirs. This is what the
believer has in his heart and mind: a sure and certain hope
that what Almighty God has promised, He is able also to
perform. This is the demonstration of the essence of faith.

Paul writes in Romans 4:17 ". . . even God, who quicken-eth the dead, and calleth those things which be not as though they were." Isn't that wonderful? He called those things which be not as though they were. You could vary these words: He called those things which be not as yet, as though they already were. It is this forward look, this expectation of the goodness and the power and the wonder-ful grace of God, that has the dynamic to inspire the life. Believing people can march forward with confidence, look-ing upward into the golden future which is theirs in the Lord Jesus Christ. If someone might say, "They are just turning away from this world," or someone else should say, "They just want an escape," it is true — they do; they really do.

So far as the believer is concerned, this is exactly what we have in mind. Does this mean he has no concern for this world? No; the concern he has is that he get out of it, and that all believers get out of it so that they can look up into the presence of the Lord. As believers in the Lord Jesus Christ they can carry this in their hearts and minds, "Let not your heart be troubled, neither let it be afraid" (John 14:27).

## Chapter 53

## SPECIAL PRIVILEGE

Do you know how a believer may accept special favors with a good conscience?

In the world there is much unfairness. Things just do not come out even. Some things are long, some are short, some are big, and some are little. There are places of advantage and there are places of disadvantage. Not every piece of pie is the same size. There are times of good fortune and there are times of bad fortune. Sometimes we speak of the wheel of fortune and we are inclined to say "round and round it goes; where it will stop, nobody knows." At times we get the breaks. Sometimes we are just lucky in the eyes of the world and I think many of us need to appreciate from time to time how fortunate we are.

As I look back over my own life I think about the privilege I had to be born in my native land, Canada. I was fortunate to be born into my family. The kind of man I had for my father, the kind of woman who was my mother, the kind of woman who was my stepmother, the kind of people who were my grandparents — for all these I am grateful. I think about the high school I attended and what an unusual situation that was; what a privilege to mingle with the boys in that school under the leadership of a fine principal. I think of all the people who have befriended me during my lifetime — what blessings have been mine.

Coming out of darkness into His marvelous light, getting to know that Jesus Christ was the Son of God, that He came into the world for me, that He died for me, and that He opened the way for me to come to God, and is even now preparing a place in heaven for me has been for me continuous blessing. The Lord told me, "In my Father's house are many mansions: if it were not so, I would have told you.

I go to prepare a place for you." I have that ahead of me. What a blessing! The churches I have attended and the believing people I have met — some well known and some obscure, some rich and some poor — what a privilege! All this has been a marvelous blessing. Receiving Christ as my Savior, receiving the Holy Spirit as my Companion, together with the opportunities I have had for service, have been a rich blessing. I look back over my life and consider how first I felt called to devote myself to the mission field. I went to the Bible Institute in Los Angeles, where I had the great privilege of studying under Dr. R. A. Torrey for two years; then I went to St. John's Presbyterian Church in Winnipeg, Manitoba, and what a privilege that was! From there I went to the Evangelical Theological College in Dallas, where there were great men of God. Later I joined the Southern Presbyterian Church. I will tell you there were giants in the land in those days among the leaders in the church. I was later called to Austin College to serve on the faculty there, and afterwards to Columbia Seminary, where I had the privilege of working and serving for twenty-seven years as Professor of English Bible and Christian Education. Now, in retirement, I am on the radio all over the country and in foreign lands. The privileges and benefits are overwhelming, and I sometimes ask myself if it is right for any one person to receive so much.

In the Exodus of the Israelites they, too, received many benefits as they traveled across the desert. As they came near to the land of Canaan the first enemy they met was King Arad of the Canaanites, whom they defeated. After taking his land, they met Sihon, king of the Amorites, and Og, king of Bashan, both of whom they defeated and whose land they seized. The result was they already occupied some land before they came to the land of Canaan.

The tribes of Reuben and Gad had a great multitude of cattle. They asked Moses for the privilege of settling on the land they had taken from these enemies. ". . . let this land be given unto thy servants for a possession" (Num. 32:5). But Moses pointed out that this could discourage the others who would still have to go over the river Jordan and enter into a country where they would have to fight a hostile enemy.

> And wherefore discourage ye the heart of the children of Israel from going over into the land which the Lord hath given them (Num. 32:7).

In conference with Moses they finally agreed on a procedure that would be fair.

> But we ourselves will go ready armed before the children of Israel, until we have brought them unto their place: and our little ones shall dwell in the fenced cities because of the inhabitants of the land. We will not return unto our houses, until the children of Israel have inherited every man his inheritance (Num. 32:17-18).

What did that mean? They would let their flocks and herds be pastured on this land, and the old men and the children would stay with the flocks and herds, while the young men who were fit for war would band together and go into the forefront of the attack in cooperation with the other tribes. They went over the river Jordan with the other tribes and fought the enemy until each tribe had been located on their own portion; then they returned home. Thus they were given special privilege but they were willing to assume special responsibility.

There is a message here for everyone who has riches. How can a person with money keep his money clean? By giving some of it to the poor. How can a person with a good education keep that from making him proud? By undertaking to work for people who do not have an education. How can a young woman who has been blessed with a beautiful face possibly enjoy her beauty without getting vain? By being kind and gracious to those not beautiful.

So we should say for ourselves: we have the Gospel. We know the Lord. We want to be blessed. How can we be blessed, so that this very knowledge will not make us proud or conceited? By sharing the Gospel with others, by teaching. Am I rejoicing in the blessing of the Lord Jesus Christ? I must do something to help others to know the Gospel or I will become careless and proud. I must help the blind man across the street; a cripple could not do it. This is how it goes! Special privilege demands special responsibility!

## Chapter 54

## GO IN AND POSSESS

Can you see there will be a time in every situation where the will of God is to be done when the believer must take action in line with the guidance he has received from God?

Salvation is the work of God. We have been saying this over and over; and we cannot say it too often. God is going to do it. God wills it. If God had planned salvation we would never have thought about it. We do not need to tell Him what to do. He actually sets it up in such a way that it will come to pass. Yet the believer must choose salvation. There is a time when he must act as he is led, if he is going to get it.

When we say salvation is the work of God, we need to remind ourselves right away He is not going to force it on anybody. He will do it, but I must receive it. He will call; I must come. He will offer it to me; I must take it. There is an aspect in this whole matter of living by faith in which the believer must commit himself. Suppose I want beans in my garden. You and I know there must be necessary preparation of the soil, and I must choose the times when this is to be done. I must buy the seed to be planted. All the preparation would be in vain unless I planted those seeds. You would be surprised how often people make plans and then do nothing.

It reminds me of what can happen sometimes when a young man and woman are seeing a lot of each other. We used to say they were courting; nowadays we talk about their going with each other. It can happen that a young fellow will go with a girl often over a period of time and they never get married. There could be one simple reason. He may never have asked her. Just going together isn't going to bring them to the result of marriage. It is as simple as that with reference to planting beans. I must drop those seeds into the ground. I must cover them and wait for them to grow. In the game of baseball, for instance, the aim is to score a run. A person going to bat may, by hitting the ball and running, eventually score a run, but when he stands there at bat, do you see he has to do something? He has to decide whether or not to strike at the ball. If he hits it, that is fine; and if he is able to get to first base before they throw him out, that is fine. But what I want to bring to our attention right now is that at that moment he is standing at the plate with the bat in his hand, with the pitcher throwing the ball; in that split second he must make up his mind: will he strike at it or will he not strike at it?

It is like that in spiritual matters. The time comes when action must be taken. You will remember it took the Israelites forty years finally to arrive at the river Jordan, poised to enter the land of Canaan. In that length of time certain things had to happen. We are considering how the Exodus of the Israelites can show us spiritual truth. We may properly have in mind that God is working always in every aspect of life, all of the time; but there comes a time when He calls you to act. He puts the situation in front of you; you have to do something. It was this way with Joshua.

> Now after the death of Moses the servant of the Lord it came to pass, that the Lord spake unto Joshua the son of Nun, Moses' minister, saying, Moses my servant is dead; now therefore arise, go over this Jordan, thou, and all this people, unto the land which I do give to them, even to the children of Israel (Jos. 1:1-2).

This is to say to Joshua, "The time is here. Moses is gone. It is now up to you and this is the time." There is much to be learned in these words spoken to Joshua.

> Every place that the sole of your foot shall tread upon, that have I given unto you, as I said unto Moses. From the wilderness and this Lebanon even unto the great river, the river Euphrates, all the land of the Hittites, and unto the Great Sea toward the going down of the sun, shall be your coast. There shall not any man be able to stand before thee all the days of

thy life: as I was with Moses, so I will be with thee:
I will not fail thee, nor forsake thee. Be strong and
of a good courage: for unto this people shalt thou
divide for an inheritance the land, which I sware unto their fathers to give them. Only be thou strong and
very courageous, that thou mayest observe to do
according to all the law, which Moses my servant
commanded thee: turn not from it to the right hand
or to the left, that thou mayest prosper whithersoever thou goest. This book of the law shall not
depart out of thy mouth; but thou shalt meditate
therein day and night, that thou mayest observe to
do according to all that is written therein: for then
thou shalt make thy way prosperous, and then thou
shalt have good success. Have not I commanded
thee? Be strong and of a good courage; be not afraid,
neither be thou dismayed: for the Lord thy God is
with thee whithersoever thou goest (Jos. 1:3-9).

These words that were spoken to Joshua can be understood as a wonderful pep talk. God is saying, "Now is the
time. You have been working as the servant of Moses. But
Moses is dead. You are the one who is going to step in there
and do it. Get up, pull yourself together." I am emphasizing
this because it is possible some of us in our spiritual experience never do "get it done." We never do swing that
bat. We never do propose to the girl, so we don't get married. I know we are not saved by works as such, but faith
of any kind that is worth anything does work. It is the work
of faith that the New Testament talks about. God called
me; He told me to come. How will I do it? He will point
out the way. It will be something I should do right in my
life. Right where I live there will be something for me to do.
He has called me and He has given me certain promises.
I have, as it were, the whole world before me, but I must
act at one point as He wills. As I am being led by the Lord,
He will be with me every step of the way. It is for me to
be obedient. "Be strong and of a good courage, fear not, nor
be afraid of them: for the Lord thy God, he it is that doth
go with thee; he will not fail thee, nor forsake thee" (Deut.
31:6). I am to act in faith, believing that when I reach out
to have something happen, God will work in me to bring it
to pass.

This is the significance of what we are thinking about just now. Let us hear the Word of the Lord: "Go in and possess the land." Whatever has been our total experience, whatever we are facing right now, whatever is hanging in the balance with us, the ball is coming up to the plate. We must make up our mind. Are we going to strike at it? The time is here to plant beans. Am I going to do it? Then let me plant beans. The idea is that somewhere, somehow, just now at this point there is something for me to do and if I will do that, God will work. My doing what is at hand will bring to pass the will of God. Thus I will actually find that as I participate and I respond and act according to the will of God, something far more than I can ask or think will happen.

## Chapter 55

## VALUE OF EXPERIENCE

If a man were driving his car recklessly at high speed and had a wreck, would he learn anything?

We often hear the expression "experience is the best teacher." I am going to raise a question by asking, is this really true? When your car ran out of gas the last time and you had to walk a mile to a telephone, what did you learn? It is possible you may have learned some specific details about that part of the road and about the hill you had to climb, and things like that of no general significance, but what was the real helpful truth that you learned? You know perfectly well you learned nothing. You had experience, but the only experience was that you found out that what you knew all the time was true.

Suppose I run into a stone wall. That hurts. Did I learn anything? You will say I learned I should not run into a stone wall. Well, didn't I already know that? I am pointing out that a great deal of the experience we have is of no value at all beyond the fact that it shows us that what we knew all the time is true. You and I can learn truth that has to do with our spiritual life without having to go through the depths. We don't have to fail in order to know that failure will follow. When the children of Israel failed to go into the promised land at Kadesh-Barnea we have noted they were turned back into the desert for thirty-eight years. What did those years contribute? Someone will say they got experience. Yes, but they did not learn one new thing. Of what use is it to live through the same situation over and over again? For instance, if a person feels weak in faith and wishes he had more faith, can you tell him what to do? I could tell him what to do without any difficulty and you could, too. The Bible will tell him. "Faith cometh by hearing, and hearing by the Word of God." (Rom. 10:17). All that person needs to do is read and study the Bible and he will have more faith. But he doesn't read the Bible, so do you know what will follow? His faith won't grow.

That is just as natural as saying that if you stay out in the rain you will get wet. There is no trick about it; and if you get out into the hot sun, you will get hot. So if you read the Bible, you could have faith. There will be no trick about that. "Faith cometh by hearing and hearing by the Word of God." The man who feels weak in faith, and is sorry he has doubts, and wishes he were not like that doesn't read. He doesn't study. For five years he doesn't study, so he still doesn't believe. For ten years he doesn't study; he still doesn't believe. In a lifetime he doesn't read and study; he will never believe. He could have known it at the beginning. We could have told him that at the outset, that "faith cometh by hearing and hearing by the Word of God." The person who doesn't read and study the Bible and doesn't hear the Gospel won't have faith.

All we are talking about is being considered in connection with salvation. Having experiences does not teach anything new, especially because those experiences only confirm in the heart and mind things already known. For instance, we have a Scripture passage that reads, "Ask and ye shall receive; seek, and ye shall find; knock, and it shall be opened unto you." Do you believe it? If a person really asked in prayer what do you think would happen? He would receive. If a person were to really seek the mind of the Lord, he would find it. If we pray, God will hear. If we don't pray, God has nothing to answer.

So we will say that if a person lives without praying, without Bible reading, without fellowship with other Christians and his faith falters, why not? That is as natural as saying that it was raining, he stayed out in the rain, the rain was cold and it became windy, but still he stayed out there; at the end of the afternoon, what would he be? He would be cold and wet. Why? Because that is where he stayed.

I don't want to make it sound too simple for you, but the matter of having fellowship with the Lord follows a pattern almost as simple as that. Those who seek His face will find it. Those who call upon Him will find Him; and to those who turn to Him, He will turn. These are things we know without first learning them by experience. There is no secret about them. If I should have an experience and I knew nothing in Scripture to guide me, how would I know what was good or bad? Because I liked it? That is not a sign anything is good. I might like poison, and the very thing I am taking because I like it might actually turn out to be wrong. No, it won't do to say that I learn by experience. I don't. Actually, experience verifies. Experience will show me some things are really true.

So we say to each other about this question "Do I need a lot of experience to become a Christian?" No. We need to understand Scripture. The more surely we know the Scriptures, the more certain we will be that we can talk to and witness to others. So I repeat, we do not need more experience in our Christian living; we need more grace. We need more help from God. Our problem is not that we don't understand His way of doing things. Our problem is that we don't *believe* His way of doing things. To strengthen our faith we need the grace of God, an inward, divine enablement that comes into our hearts and strengthens us to believe the things that are true about the Lord; and in this way we can learn.

## Chapter 56

## CANAAN, THE LAND OF PROMISE

Do you realize that the power of the Gospel comes from its promise of better things to come, of a glorious future?

We have reminded ourselves over and over that salvation is the work of God. It is God who does it. In order for us to learn more about it we have looked into the Scriptures to see illustrations of salvation which God has given there, the demonstrations of salvation that He has given in the sacred history of His people. We have learned that, so far as the children of Israel were concerned, their experience in being led out of Egypt across the desert into Canaan is a marvelous description of the work of God. It is actually a representation of the whole course of salvation.

The children of Israel were slaves in Egypt. They didn't belong there, and they were not going to stay there. The land of Canaan had been promised to them by God in His dealing with Abraham. This work of salvation God developed and carried out in what we commonly call the Exodus of Israel.

Salvation as shown in Scripture, and as worked out by the Lord Jesus Christ is operative in us in all three tenses of human experience: past, present, and future. When I come to God through Christ Jesus, I love to think I can come "just as I am without one plea, but that thy blood was shed for me." When I say I am coming just as I am, how am I? Who is this "I" that is coming? I have a past. I have lived. I have done things. I have failed and have not done things I should have done. I have sinned against God. There is no possible way in which I can change any part of that. This is the glorious "but": but Christ Jesus died for me. He carried away my sins. He is able to blot out my transgressions. He casts all my sins behind Him; I am forgiven. Praise the Lord! It is also true about this "I" in "Just as I am" that I have a present, right now. I am living in this world just as I am: weak, ignorant, many times perverse. When I say "just as I am" I mean just like that. What is my hope, then, when I come to God? Do you know what is happening to give me confidence in coming? Christ Jesus is interceding for me.

John wrote his first epistle that I should not sin, but then he tells me that if I do sin I have an advocate with the Father, even Jesus Christ, the Righteous. I have the Savior of all mankind, the Son of God interceding on my behalf right now in the presence of God. In other words, I am now being helped. I am now being kept. Praise the Lord! Now He is taking care of me.

But there is something else: I have a future. I am going to live by His grace all the days of my life, and when I am through with this world I am going into His presence. My heart need not be worried, neither need it be afraid, because in my Father's house there are many mansions. If it were not so, He would have told me. He has gone to prepare one for me, even though I do not deserve it. As I move forward into His presence I aim to be doing His will — faulty, imperfect, often sinning, many times careless. I should be ashamed of myself, but just the same, He is on my side.

Living in the land as the children of Israel did meant living in the promises of God. That is how the believer can live. What wonderful promises we have! Listen to this: "I will never leave thee nor forsake thee." Can you believe it? Isn't that wonderful? "I will be with thee whithersoever thou goest." Think of it. "I will hold thy right hand, saying unto thee, Fear not; I will help thee." What more could we ask for? "Whosoever believeth in Him shall not perish but have eternal life." There are many more. Believers are counting on those promises.

The Israelites were promised that God would be with them when they reached the land of Canaan. The land of Canaan had been promised to Abraham and to his seed, but there was a situation in the land of Canaan that I think we are often inclined to overlook. That land of Canaan was occupied. Even so with us, there are spiritual forces and factors against us that are evil. If I intend to walk with the Lord, there are those who will be against me. "The devil walketh about as a roaring lion seeking whom he may devour." When coming into the promises of God the forces of Satan are there and they are evil; their control of the spiritual world is real and I will have to wrest it from them. The promises of God will only be gained as I contend with these forces in high places. There will be the high walled cities of "Custom"; and the giant soldiers of "Opposition" will be against me. Just as Israel needed to conquer the land by defeating the enemy who occupied it, so I must conquer my place, my privilege in the promises of God, by defeating those who oppose me.

I am personally unable. I am weak. I am not equipped. But I have the promises of God, and He will be with me; and as Joshua and Caleb told the children of Israel, "Our God shall fight for us. If God be for us, who can be against us?" The Israelites were to proceed by faith. All along one principle was to prevail, which bears repeating. So far as the promises of God were concerned, "every place that the sole of your foot shall tread upon, that have I given you as I said to Moses." I must put my weight upon it. I must step out there and put my foot on it, and if I trust in the promises of God and depend on them, He will glorify His name. He will show Himself able.

Canaan is indeed the land of the promises of God. It is the promised land so far as you and I are concerned. We have the privilege and the expectation of living every day and tomorrow in the promises of God.

## Chapter 57

## ISRAEL THE PEOPLE OF GOD

Do you understand that Israel in the Old Testament was to be an example to the whole world of what it means to live in faith?

It is a common thing to refer to the Israelites in the Old Testament as "the chosen people." I think this particular expression has baffled and disturbed some and has been misunderstood many times. Because Israel was thought of as the chosen people there has been the chance that some would think them proud, or that they felt themselves to be better than others. I taught school for a number of years and sometimes I would encourage my students to take physical exercises. In order to get them to take exercises I would have to teach them how to exercise and train them in the postures they were to take, in the positions their bodies should be in. Suppose I were instructing them in a matter of raising and lowering their arms. Can you understand how I would take one pupil who seemed to be more apt perhaps than others and I would say to him, "Let me use you to show these people." When he would come forward before the class, I would tell him, "Raise your arm." When he had done this I might say, "The right arm should be higher and the left a little lower. You should keep your thumb next to the forefinger. Turn your hands a little, now let them down." Thus by using this boy as an example I taught the whole class what I meant. In that sense the boy was "chosen" to be an example. He would still have to pass the examination the class as a whole would have. So God "chose" the family of Abraham and Isaac and then of Jacob, to be a company of people who would show to the whole world what a company of people should do in walking in faith in God.

The Israelites were not always successful. When they made a mistake, He showed what He does to anyone who makes a mistake. He never did cast them off, but He stayed with them and found ways of correcting and forgiving them. When I was teaching, many times I would seek to get all the students to show what this example did for them.

The Israelites were the chosen people of God, not because they were better than other people. They were the same kind of folks as others. What happened to them was all under the control of God and He used their experiences to show His ways to other people. We find this in I Corinthians 10:11: "Now all these things happened unto them for examples: (and the context makes it plain he is talking about Israel) and they are written for our admonition, upon whom the ends of the world are come."

In revealing the truth about the work of God in salvation through Jesus Christ, Israel was used as the authentic example of the people of God. The story begins with Israel in Egypt, God's people in this world. They were not to stay in Egypt. That was not the land that was promised to them. They were eventually to live in the land of Canaan. Bringing them out of Egypt into Canaan was an illustration of God coming to me in the flesh and calling me into the Spirit. Israel experienced deliverance. That is a great word. That meant getting Israel out of Egypt in order to be blessed. Israel would never have the blessing of God in Egypt. What does that mean for us? We will never have the blessing of God in this world. We may be prospered in this world but that will not be the prime result of belonging to the Lord.

The second thing I want to point out about the Israelites in the Exodus is that they were directed. In the course of their journeying they did not have to figure out where to go. They did not have to scout around and conjecture and make a program to see if it would work. They were led by a cloud by day and a pillar of fire by night, an indication that the Lord was their constant companion and guide.

The cloud in the daytime provided shade and the fire in the night gave them light. They were taught by object lessons of experience in their journey. The Lord led them through the experience of bitter water that was made sweet. He led them through the experience of hunger and then sent them the manna from heaven. He led them through the experience of having thirst and then having water gush from the rock. They had the experience of conflict, when Amalek was about to defeat them, and then united inter-cessory prayer won the victory. They had the problem of human limitations and this was solved by organization.

All of these things the people of Israel were taught. They were not just told it would be this way; they were led through experiences, the Lord showing them His way. They came to Mt. Sinai, and there they were trained. The law, the Ten Commandments, was laid out before them there. The pattern of the tabernacle was set up before them, and the order in which they were to march was put before them. They were disciplined: when they did wrong they were punished. Failure to obey brought judgment from God. On occasion, when they murmured against God, a plague would strike them until Moses would pray for them. In the case of Kadesh-Barnea, when they provoked God, He sent them back into the desert until all of that generation died. He did not forsake them but they did not receive the blessing. God was faithful to them in spite of their failure to obey Him.

This is one of the wonderful things about God that is revealed in connection with the children of Israel. Moses reminded them that they were not better than others. He said in effect, "Look and see about yourselves. You are not so many. There are other tribes that are more numerous than you. You were not chosen because you were many, and you were not chosen because you were strong, and you were not chosen because you were good, and you were not chosen because you were so faithful; because in all these things you fell short. You were chosen because God wanted the world to know about His ways of dealing with His people. He used you to show the whole world the way He has of doing things."

As we come toward the end of Israel's experience we find they were brought through to victory despite their failure, and despite all the problems they had. They finally entered into the land where they were to have the fullness of blessing. Under the leadership of Joshua and others they continued to live that way until they were brought through into full possession of the land. There at the River Jordan they were led across into full victory in the land of the promises of God.

This is the story of Israel, the people of God. Have you felt that it is your story, too? That is exactly how it will go with you. He will find you, wherever you are, and He will lead you through all manner of experiences to Himself. The joy of the Lord now and in the years to come can be your great treasure, your precious possession, when you belong to Him.

## Chapter 58

## JOSHUA, THE LEADER FROM GOD

Have you ever considered the importance of the work of a leader in salvation?

We understand by the word "salvation" everything that God does in and for and through the human being who believes in the Lord Jesus Christ by the grace of God. It is something that originated with God, and He brings it to pass. But it operates in man. Salvation takes place in a human being. It operates by the response of man to the guidance of God. God shows man what He wants man to do, and He enables the willing man to do it. In salvation the soul is not taken out of this world into another place that has better conditions. The work of God is done in the individual, in the world, as that individual responds to the will of God here and now.

When the Lord Jesus Christ wanted His disciples to remember Him, He took bread, and when He brake it He said, "This is my body broken for you; take, eat in remembrance of me." How is the eating done? By each individual. That bread goes in one mouth at a time. "This cup is the New Testament in my blood shed for many for the remission of sins. Drink ye all of it." How is the drinking done? One person at a time. That is the way the Gospel comes to you. The work of God in salvation is done in the individual as that individual responds to the will of God. Since the will of God is often obscure, what is a man going to do in responding to God? Here is a young person who wants to do the will of God. How would he know? How would he do it? It is a fact that a believer who has just turned to God needs help from someone who knows the way.

Since the plan of God is to save by His Son, it is fitting

that His Son should reveal how it is done. Jesus of Nazareth, while He was here, did reveal in His death and in His resurrection and ascension into heaven how the work of God is done. Believers are to be as little children. Except they be as little children they will not enter the kingdom of heaven. Now, if they are going to be as little children, someone is to lead them and that is one of the lovely representations of the grace of God. "For I the Lord thy God will hold thy right hand, saying unto thee, Fear not; I will help thee" (Isa. 41:13).

In the history of Israel again and again God would raise up a leader, as He raised up Moses and afterwards Joshua. Moses led the people out of Egypt, across the desert, and Joshua led the people into the promised land. Later on this happened over and over. David was the great king and led his people. There were prophets like Elijah, Elisha, Isaiah, and Amos, who led the people into an understanding of the ways of God. Moses is considered, perhaps, the typical, outstanding leader. We read in Deuteronomy that the people asked Moses to represent them to God. The people indicated to Moses they were afraid to come into the presence of God personally because they didn't know how to act. Moses then taught the people what the will of God was.

We have apostles, evangelists, pastors, and teachers in the New Testament. We think of Paul when we think of the New Testament. You remember, too, the words said about John the Baptist: "There was a man sent from God whose name was John." Let me draw your attention to some of the qualifications such leaders would need. You may wonder, "What bearing does that have on me?" In some measure you will be a leader for somebody. Are you a parent? Well, you are certainly a leader. Are you an older brother or sister, are you a believer in your church or Sunday School? You have a responsibility for leading other people to God. The leader needs personal experience in faith. In this connection we think of Paul.

> Howbeit for this cause I obtained mercy, that in me first Jesus Christ might show forth all long-suffering, for a pattern to them which should hereafter believe on him to life everlasting (I Tim. 1:16).

Thus the leader himself experiences it. Moses knew about God. And so he could lead the other people. Martin Luther was a great leader who personally experienced what it was to come to know Christ Jesus as his Savior and Lord and to be justified by faith. Because he knew personally what it meant, he could teach others.

And so I would like to say to you: do you have personal faith in God? If you do, it will show through. As surely as you have it, you will be used of God in leading others. It was always important that a leader should be a veteran, one who had experienced the things of the Lord. Paul could say, speaking of himself:

> I know both how to be abased, and I know how to abound: every where and in all things I am instructed both to be full and to be hungry, both to abound and to suffer need (Phil. 4:12).

This was the kind of man who could lead and teach others. For all his experiences, he was not vain. He realized that he was unable in himself to do the will of God. He realized he had no strength of his own, which led him to add these words: "I can do all things through Christ who strengtheneth me" (Phil. 4:13).

If you are a mother or father, and you now feel helpless about doing anything for your child, let me ask this, "Are you depending on yourself or are you depending on Christ?" If you would depend on the Lord you would not need to have strength in yourself. All that you would need is to be strong in faith, committing yourself to Him. The Lord would do for you whatever might be needed.

The leader must also be commissioned for the task. He must have some sense of the fact the Lord wants him to lead. That was the way it was with Moses and Joshua. These men were called, instructed, and commissioned in a rather dramatic fashion. When David was to be made king he was commissioned with anointing by Samuel. In our day no one like Samuel is here to anoint us, and we may not have the same kind of experience as Moses had when he was at the burning bush, but we can have our own personal dealings with God. When we are commissioned for a task it is important to understand that this is the way God wants it. We are to exercise our faith in God.

At a certain point when Moses was distressed and went to God wondering what he was to do when facing the Red Sea, God asked him, "What is that in thine hand? Take that rod and use it and smite the water and it will open up before you." Moses had to exercise his own faith in order to bring the people through to the blessing. In similar fashion a parent, friend, pastor, or personal worker must exercise his own faith.

With reference to the Galatians, the apostle Paul said that he was experiencing the pangs of birth all over again, the second time, in seeking to bring them to God in their continuing walk with the Lord. Thus we realize that the leader called of God is prepared of God, because each one in his own way is an example of our Lord and Savior Jesus Christ, who personally saves us by His grace and mercy.

## Chapter 59

## RIVER JORDAN

Are you prepared to think that a crisis may arise while you are obeying God?

There is no doubt that God is always the same. He is constant. If everything were as God would have it, we would not have any unusual circumstances. We would have no such thing as a crisis. We would never be in trouble, because God would do all things well. But the situation is such that in this world it is not like that. Our need for grace is constant. We are not strong enough, nor wise enough, nor good enough to manage to do what needs to be done. We need His grace to know which way to go and where to go. We need His grace to be able to go, to have it in us to go. Even so, our course of experience is not smooth. Even when walking in obedience we can run into obstructions. We move along and the first thing we know it is as if the doors were shut, and we do not know what to do next. This causes a crisis.

Situations can develop that will challenge decisive action and if we once decide to go a certain way we are committed to it. We cannot go back. For instance, it is as if I were making up my mind whether or not I should cut down a certain tree. What makes this issue so important is that when once that tree is cut down, the situation is settled.

When I am facing an issue and wondering what to do, that is what I am calling a crisis. I know that everything is in the Lord's hands, but it may be in His will to challenge me to act. He may place me in a situation where I must make up my mind about something. It can happen that such a crisis may thwart my progress. I have to face it. The history of Israel affords several such vivid experiences. When the people of Israel were leaving Egypt they came to one big barrier that was almost insurmountable: the Red Sea was in front of them. This was a crisis. What could they do? And again when they had wandered in the desert for forty years they came to the River Jordan. The river was in flood and it was absolutely impossible for them to get across. Here again was a crisis.

These situations could be similar to what happens when a believer is considering total surrender to the Lord. It seems to be true that a person can believe in Christ Jesus as Savior, and yet not yield to Him as the Lord of his life. A person can trust in Jesus Christ to save his soul, and at the same time live his life the way he thinks would be good in his own opinion. I shall not judge that person. You may wonder whether I would call him a Christian. I would not call him anything. I would let the Lord judge him. That is the Lord's business. I am only saying now that such is possible.

There are people who have started walking with the Lord, seeking His face, having fellowship with Him, and for one reason or another have then started walking on their own. They are not really being led by the Lord. We can be sure such a person is not happy. That person is not blessed, and many times he has no victory. Inside himself, he has no power in prayer, in overcoming evil. He has no power to resist his own peculiar temptations, and he has no communion with the Lord. He may tell you that Jesus is Lord and that He came to die for sinners. He may tell you that he personally is a sinner, but you will not see in his face the glow of personal fellowship with the Lord. There is in his heart and in his spirit no liberty to witness. He does not want to talk about the Lord. He has no interest in missions or evangelism. There is no deliverance from addiction on his part; he may be given over to something that has him enslaved and from which he cannot escape.

About whom am I talking? I am talking about a person who believes in God and in Jesus Christ, but who has not yet yielded himself to the living Lord. For him something needs to happen. We may gain insight by again considering Israel. When the children of Israel were coming out of

Egypt, Joshua after Moses' ministry was finished, led the people to the River Jordan. There he took steps to make the crossing a memorable occasion. He arranged that priests should gather stones from the bank of the river and when they crossed the Jordan they were to place these stones on the bottom and there build an altar in that very riverbed. Anybody in the future looking down there would wonder how those stones got there, and it would cause people to say, "One day the children of Israel crossed over here on dry land and they built that altar with stones from the hill over yonder." Joshua also had the priests pick up certain stones from the bottom of the river, worn smooth with the flowing of the water, carry them to the top of the hill and there build an altar to let all the world know that the children of Israel had passed through the River Jordan. In these ways this great event was to be remembered.

There was no bridge over the Jordan, and once over the river the Israelites were committed to being aliens in a strange land. This was a dangerous situation, and Joshua knew it would be wonderful for them if they could remember that God had led them to that place and that He would keep them there. They would face problems but there were none that God could not solve. By reason of an agreement made with Moses two tribes, Reuben and Gad, did not need to cross the river. Many Bible students find this crossing of the Jordan a sign of a second blessing. They point out that the Israelites crossed the Red Sea first at the beginning of their journeys, and then crossed the River Jordan at the end of their journey. Thus this could be taken to indicate a second blessing. Some Bible students will speak of receiving Jesus of Nazareth as Savior and then later receiving Christ Jesus as Lord. Thus there would be a first and a second blessing in the course of spiritual experience. There may be an element of truth in what they are intimating. It seems to be true that a person may commit himself to God, believing in the Lord Jesus Christ, and thus be blessed by Him. Then as days go by, the Spirit may bring more truth into the heart so that person may suddenly realize that the Lord Jesus Christ wants to have daily fellowship with him. When that realization becomes clear and real it can be a marvelous experience. It is often an experience of rededication, an experience of consecration.

It is possibly true that some people like Reuben and Gad do not need to have a vivid second experience of having to receive the Holy Spirit as if that were a separate thing. This could depend on how they had been taught. The fullness of blessing can come to those who commit themselves definitely to total obedience whenever that is done. That is what the children of Israel did when they crossed the River Jordan. They were going over one time and would never come back. There were no bridges to burn behind them. So it is for those of us who walk with the Lord. We yield ourselves to Him and take His hand in ours, and we are with Him from then on. We have every reason to rejoice in His presence for the rest of our days.

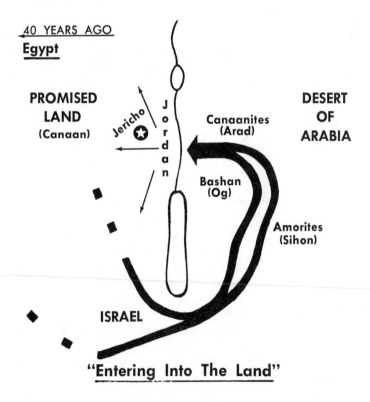

"Entering Into The Land"

## Chapter 60

## PROMISE OF BLESSING

Have you realized that it is the will of God that His creatures should enjoy His bounty and His grace?

All of our studies have been grouped around the general theme — the salvation of God. We have said that God is the Savior. Salvation is the work of God, and we have kept in mind that this work takes place in a human being. The human being is not made into an angel, but his condition can be changed. This human being — a person such as you and I — is capable of joy, gladness, and satisfaction in the same way he was capable of unhappiness, sadness, and distress. Man seeks well-being, and can delight in the relationships he has. We try to enter into a certain relationship with the physical world so that we can be comfortable and have enough to eat. We enter into a certain relationship with the social world in order to live with people and have friends. We can enter into a certain relationship in the spiritual world that we may have the favor of God.

The natural man works to secure all of these needs by his wits, by his wisdom, and by his work. This was shown early in the Bible, in Genesis. We read how a whole generation of people got together and said, ". . . let us make brick . . . let us build us a city and a tower . . . let us make us a name, lest we be scattered." Thus the men of Babel made the classic attempt to secure the values of living that they might live well because they were able to build something that would stand like the Tower of Babel. But the Lord scattered them abroad upon the face of the earth. By way of contrast, Abraham looked for a city which hath foundations whose builder and maker is God.

We find in the vision that John had in Revelation that he

saw the kingdom of God coming down from heaven as a bride adorned for her husband. That vision revealed that a city came down which is a structure of human relationships. The whole arrangement was in God's plan. This is the classic route to success in living. Abraham believed God would do what He promised. He wanted cattle, wealth, good health — all of the things the men of Babel wanted, but he wanted God to give them to him. I have always been blessed to read the incident in the career of Abraham when he delivered the people of Sodom from the enemy, and when he restored the King of Sodom with his people to his own city. The king tried to give him something but Abraham would not accept it. This did not mean that Abraham was not interested in having things, but he was determined that God should get the glory.

So the record shows that Abraham looked for a city which hath foundations, whose builder and maker is God. He expected to reach that city and counted himself in this world like a stranger and a pilgrim. He was just traveling through. This promise was to Abraham and to his seed. We are his seed, as we believe in the same way Abraham believed. This is the plan of God for eternity. This is what He always had in mind. He had in mind that His Son would be the firstborn among many brethren and this is the way those brethren would be gained.

The actual history of mankind comes to mind at this time and we will remember how man was made in the image of God and put in the Garden of Eden, how man sinned in making a selfish choice, how sin entered into man's affairs and into man's life and ruined him, defiled and snared him, so that he was doomed. "The soul that sinneth it shall die." Then we remember the grace of God, how "God so loved the world that He gave His only begotten Son that whosoever believeth in Him should not perish but have everlasting life." And so the whole world was treated to an exhibition of the grace of God that even to this day the angels cannot fully understand. "God commended His love toward us in that while we were yet sinners, Christ died for the ungodly." This is a tremendous thing.

The book of Revelation indicates to us that the angels

desired to look into this very thing. It is a mystifying thing in heaven to this day. Why would God send His own Son into this world to die for sinners? The answer is in the grace of God. A letter came to me asking this question: how could I understand, or how could I believe that Jesus Christ went to the cross to die in view of the fact that He was perfect? This, of course, shows that the human heart cannot understand it at all. We need to have spiritual insight and grace to be able to accept this remarkable truth.

Strange as it may be, the whole truth is He loves us and gave Himself for us. He died for our sins so that we could be free and be with Him forever. He took away our sins and set us free.

Now, with all that we have said about salvation, basing our interpretation upon the Exodus of Israel, you may possibly have the feeling within yourself that you would never be able to remember everything that has been said. I realize that. Just keep in mind that this is what the Bible is about — to explain how it was possible that Almighty God would arrange for our salvation. Every time you read and study the Scriptures you will remember more. We are not worthy. We are not fit. We are not even fit after He calls us, but He knows what He is doing, and His grace is sufficient for us.

Christ Jesus died for our sins and so it is true to this day that "whosoever believeth in Him shall not perish but have everlasting life." This is the salvation of God.